52 WEEKLY Devotions for FAMILY PRAYER

Karen Whiting

ROSEKIDZ®

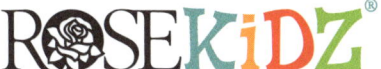

52 Weekly Devotions for Family Prayer
Copyright © 2021 Karen Whiting

Published by RoseKidz®
RoseKidz is a division of Tyndale House Ministries
Rose Publishing, LLC
P.O. Box 3473
Peabody, Massachusetts 01961-3473 USA
www.hendricksonpublishinggroup.com

All rights reserved.

Managing Editor: Karen McGraw
Assistant Editor: Talia Messina

Interior layout by Talia Messina
Front cover design by Drew McCall
Back cover design by Talia Messina

No part of this work may be reproduced or transmitted in any form or by any means, electronic or mechanical, including photocopying, recording, or by any information storage and retrieval system, without permission in writing from the publisher.

Scripture quotations are taken from the Holy Bible, New Living Translation, copyright © 1996, 2004, 2015 by Tyndale House Foundation. Used by permission of Tyndale House Publishers, Inc., Carol Stream, Illinois 60188. All rights reserved.

Published in association with Books & Such Literary Management, 52 Mission Circle #122, PMB 170, Santa Rosa, CA 95409, www.booksandsuch.com.

ISBN: 978-1-64938-026-5
#L50051
RoseKidz Reorder #380265
JUVENILE NONFICTION/Religious/Christian/Devotional & Prayer

Printed in the United States of America
Printed July 2021

Dedication

Dedicated to prayer warriors among my family and friends including:

- Rebecca and Pastor Larry White
- Darlene and Frank Pena
- Mira and Herb Pena
- My mastermind group: Deb DeArmond, Linda Gilden, Linda Goldfarb, Amy Hardoon, Melissa Henderson, Yvonne Ortega, Rhonda Robinson, PeggySue Wells, and Debbie W. Wilson.

Table of Contents

Dear Parents..7
Family Prayer Benefits and Tips...8
Week 1: What Is Prayer?..17
Week 2: What Iis Worship?..21
Week 3: What Is Sin?...25
Week 4: What Does God Do for Me?...29
Week 5: Does It Help to Pray for Other People? 33
Week 6: How Did Jesus Pray?..37
Week 7: What Is Daily Bread? 41
Week 8: Does God See My Tears?..45
Week 9: How Soon Will God Answer My Prayer? 49
Week 10: How Can I Praise God?..53
Week 11: What Happens When I Pray with My Family?............57
Week 12: How Do I Bless Someone?...61
Week 13: When Should I Pray for Someone Else? 65
Week 14: Why Does God Let People Do Bad Things?...............69
Week 15: How Strong Is God? 73
Week 16: How Do I Know God's Will?......................................77
Week 17: Can God Help Me Stop Worrying? 81
Week 18: How Can I Stop My Anger? 85
Week 19: How Does God Help Me Solve Problems?..................89
Week 20: How Does Forgiveness Help Me?...............................93
Week 21: Is a Short Prayer Okay?..97
Week 22: What Prayers Are in the Bible?.................................101
Week 23: Can God Help Me with Bullies?...............................105
Week 24: Can I Trust God?..109

Week 25: What's a Prayer Buddy?...113
Week 26: How Is Singing like Praying? 117
Week 27: What If I Don't Know What to Pray? 121
Week 28: What Is the Fear of the Lord?...125
Week 29: What Can God Do? 129
Week 30: What Is a Prayer Walk? 133
Week 31: What Does God Want Me to Do Today? 137
Week 32: How Do I Thank God?...141
Week 33: Does God Help When I Hurt? 145
Week 34: Why Should I Journal? 149
Week 35: Should I Keep Praying?...153
Week 36: What's the "Golden Rule"? 157
Week 37: Why Is Truth Important? 161
Week 38: Can Prayer Help Me Change?..165
Week 39: How Do My Prayers Help Others? 169
Week 40: How Does Praying Together Give Us Power? 173
Week 41: How Can I Hear God? 177
Week 42: Where Is God When I'm Scared?..181
Week 43: How Is God like a Rock? 185
Week 44: How Can I Make God Smile? 189
Week 45: Am I Important to God?..193
Week 46: What Is a Blessing? 197
Week 47: Can God Help Us Stop Fighting? 201
Week 48: How Can I Learn about God? 205
Week 49: How Can I Share My Faith? 209
Week 50: What Does "Glory to God" Mean?..213
Week 51: What Should I Do When God Answers My Prayers? 217
Week 52: What Does It Mean to Commit to God? 221

Dear Parents,

> **Where two or three people gather together as my followers, I am there among them.**
>
> **Matthew 18:20**

Family devotions became the foundation and continual help for our family with five children. It helped us stay close during many military deployments knowing Dad read the same devotional we used at home.

Let family time be exciting. Laugh together, enjoy hands-on activities to investigate truths, and reinforce concepts about prayer. Celebrate prayer answers and persist in long-term prayer needs.

Each week includes a different family prayer method to try. See which ones work best for your family as you discover that God listens and responds to your prayers. A family prayer journal really helps you look back together to see God's faithfulness and how devotions developed faith and family bonds. Journal prompts can help you add thoughts and responses from the week to create a written memory of your prayer journey.

The chats and Scriptures help you dig in and discuss topics so you can go deeper, according to the ages of your children.

Blessings,
Karen Whiting

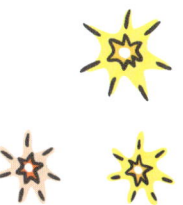

Family Prayer Benefits and Tips

HOW: Start Simple

S   Schedule time to gather together

I   Involve your children and chat to dive deeper into each topic

M   Mix in fun and hands-on experiences

P   Plan ahead and choose what you'll do before each week starts

L   Let it become a legacy with capturing the memories

E   End each one with prayer

Be Ready and Willing to Go the Distance

- Be committed
- Be consistent
- Be enthusiastic
- Be flexible
- Be realistic and understand your child's ability
- Be open-minded to children's responses (and guide them to truth)
- Be in the Word yourself so you know the Bible

Benefits of Family Prayer

There are many spiritual and cognitive benefits of praying and understanding elements of prayer. Here is a short list:

- Connects children to God and helps them talk to God
- Maintains the role of parents as the spiritual leaders of their families
- Strengthens family bonds
- Focuses on God's best for us
- Helps children see that God answers prayers
- Helps families develop grateful hearts and fear of the Lord
- Helps children learn to talk with adults
- Develops reading comprehension and vocabulary
- Develops analytical skills
- Brings your family together on a regular basis
- Gives children hope
- Helps children understand that God guides them

> *Confess your sins to each other and pray for each other so that you may be healed. The earnest prayer of a righteous person has great power and produces wonderful results.*
> **James 5:16**

Do Family Prayer Devotions Your Way!

These are really do-votions. It's a combination of a devotion, hands-on activities, and topics to chat about. It gets you actively doing things as you study God's Word.

Your family can decide your level of commitment each week. Some weeks are harder than others. You might only have time to read the devotion and maybe do a few chats in the car or put out supplies for family members to do an activity as they have time. Let it fit your lifestyle.

Prayer Journal

Build a scrapbook prayer journal with artwork and notes as you gather together. This can be a simple notebook where you write down prayer requests and praise reports. You could even use an empty photo album and write notes on index cards.

Celebrate Your Time Together

Commit to one time a week as the launch day for family devotions (that may actually vary) and one time to wrap it up. Let the rest be options to choose a la carte. Sometimes you can do it all, and some weeks may get so busy that you can only do a little.

Celebrate what you do get done. Remember that ten minutes a day, six days a week, adds up to a whole hour of family prayer time. Baby steps are better than nothing, so do your best!

Choose Your Family Style

Start the devotionals at the beginning of the year, the week you buy the book, or whatever time works best for your family. Begin with:

- an activity to introduce the concept and then read the devotions, or
- the devotion, or
- a Scripture and Chat Prompt, and then add what looks doable that week.

If One Parent or Guardian Has a Job That Includes Frequent Travel:

- Buy two copies of this book—one copy for family at home and one book (or downloadable book) for the family member who is away.
- Record sessions the traveling family member misses.
- Do some Activity Options online or video call to stay connected.
- Take lots of photos or video chat to bridge the distance for the member who is away.
- Let the absent family member email about the week's topic.

Each Prayer Devotion Week Includes:

- One devotion to read and reflect on together
- Three optional activities
- Bible Story Connection of a Bible passage to read and explore
- Three chat prompts paired with a Scripture to promote discussion
- Three ideas to add art to the prayer journal
- One family prayer method to try
- Wrap up to sum up and close the week

How to Use This Book

Activities and Chat Prompts

Don't feel like you need to do every activity every week. Choose what works. You can always go through the book again in a year or two and use different activities.

Bible Story Connection

Part of doing devotions as a family is studying God's truth in the Bible. Make this exploration fun by engaging all the senses. Act out stories, retell them, and consider how to bring in aromas and sounds associated with each story.

Prayer Journal Options

Transform the prompts into a keepsake that will help your family reflect and remember each week. You can buy a special book to journal in and add photos, or just staple sheets of paper together. Each week look for the suggestions of how to reflect and add memories to your scrapbook.

- Let children add dabs of watercolor, a drawing, or stamp design.
- Write in words that became buzz words during the week.
- Add fun stickers that relate to the week's theme.
- Take photos of your family doing the activities and add them to the scrapbook.
- Jazz it up as desired to express how your family responded to the topic.

Prayer

Use the prayer throughout the week. Make copies and keep them handy for on-the-go moments. Keep track of prayer requests and answered prayers in your scrapbook/journal.

Wrap-Up

End each week with a brief time to chat about the topic and activities. Ask what each person learned and add those thoughts to the pages of your scrapbook/journal.

Start (or Restart) Any Week!

Don't wait for a new year to start family devotions. Start this week. Any time of year is a great time to start:

- Easter and new hope
- Spring and planting seed of faith
- Summer with a less rigid calendar
- Fall and the start of school
- Christmas or the New Year for new birth and new starts

1. As parents, read the "Dear Parents" letter and the introduction.
2. If this is a restart, or you need motivation to persist, read the list of benefits and select the three top reasons you want to succeed at family devotions. Post those somewhere very visible for your family. Let those be your motivation or mottos to keep going.
3. Turn to the current week and get going!

Get Kids Excited about Devotions

1. Talk the devotions up.
Bring the devotion ideas into family meal times and drive times. Chat about the Scriptures, talks, and activities. Pray at all opportunities.

2. Capture the fun in pictures.
Be sure to take photos of the activities when possible and build a family memory keepsake by adding the suggested art, thoughts, and photos to the scrapbook/prayer journal.

3. Engage the senses.
Use visuals and sounds affiliated with stories to deepen the impact. Act out passages. Why not cook foods that relate to Bible times or themes? This helps children experience and understand Bible times. For more food ideas see *The Family Cookbook Devotional: 50 Recipes for Faith, Food, and Fun* at hendricksonrose.com/rosekidz.

4. Pray with a prayer cup.
Decorate a plastic cup with permanent makers. Cut slips of paper and write the names of each family member on one. At the end of each devotion, let each member draw a name to pray for that person. Or you can have someone draw one name at a meal and then, as a family, pray for that individual. If desired, add names of other family members and friends to pray for them.

5. Connect with one-on-one time.
Consider doing some activities with one child at a time. Children love this special bonding time with a parent or guardian.

6. Memorize the week's opening Scripture.
Read the verse daily and talk about what it means. After a few days, say some of the words and see if they can finish the verse. Recite it together. Look up fun memory verse games online.

7. Provide each child with their own age-appropriate Bible.
Having their own Bibles helps increase their interest. You can also provide journals or prayer notebooks. Match these items to your children's ages and learning styles. Visual learners want more pictures and charts; analytical children enjoy charts and facts; social learners like profiles about people and places.

8. Share what you learn.
Invite friends to join you for some of the devotions. Share the memories and how the devotion time helps your family grow in faith and other areas.

What Is Prayer?

Week 1

Family Beatitude: Happy is the family who understands prayer, for they know God listens.

Focus: Understanding prayer

Weekly Bible Verse: *Look! I stand at the door and knock. If you hear my voice and open the door, I will come in, and we will share a meal together as friends.* Revelation 3:20

Activity Options

- ☐ Prayer is spending time connecting with God, talking and listening. Do some connect-the-dot puzzles to discover the picture. Discuss how prayer helps us know God.
- ☐ Make a doorknob hanger with words that welcome Jesus.
- ☐ Write a prayer to God. Start with the greeting, "Dear _____."

Learning to Talk 2 minutes

"Mommy! Billy said 'Dada.'" Jenna squealed as she played with her little brother.

"He's learning to talk." Mommy smiled.

"What was my first word?"

"Duck. You loved feeding the ducks. You would grab oats in your hands and run down the hill yelling 'Duck, duck.' The ducks would waddle to you and eat as oats fell out of your hands. Then you'd sit and the ducks gathered around you."

"That's funny."

"You were so excited to see them. God wants us to be that excited when we pray. He loves to hear you call his name."

"When did I start to pray?"

"We prayed over you every night and at meals like we do now. One day you started to clap as we folded our hands to pray. Then you started to repeat phrases we said, like 'God bless,' 'thank you,' and 'amen.'"

"I'm still learning more about how to talk to God and to stop and listen."

Bible Story Connection 3–4 minutes

Read Nehemiah 1:5-11. Discuss what Nehemiah said to honor God, confess, show he knew God, and what asked for.

Chat Prompts

- *When Moses came down Mount Sinai carrying the two stone tablets inscribed with the terms of the covenant, he wasn't aware that his face had become radiant because he had spoken to the LORD.* Exodus 34:29

    Moses had such a close prayer life with God that his face shone. He lit up! Talk about what gets you excited about praying.

- *When you pray, don't babble on and on as the Gentiles do. They think their prayers are answered merely by repeating their words again and again.* Matthew 6:7

    Discuss how we don't need big words or to impress God. What do you need?

- *Search for the LORD and for his strength; continually seek him.* 1 Chronicles 16:11

    What does this verse remind us about prayer?

MORE TIME?

Prayer Journal Options

Make a memory about what you read, did, and learned this week.

- Nehemiah prayed for his country. Write one for your country.
- Write your first words and some new words to God.
- Draw body parts and write prayers for each picture (see below).

Family Prayer: Head to Toe

Pray for God to help you with each part of you. As you read the prayer list below, touch each corresponding body part, then read the verse.

- Give me the mind of Jesus; 1 Corinthians 2:16
- Guide my eyes to seek you and opportunities to help others; Matthew 6:22
- Open my ears to listen and obey; Luke 11:28
- Help me open my mouth with kindness and praise; Ephesians 4:29
- Fill my heart with love for everyone you created, and also for you; Luke 6:45-46
- Help me use my hands for good works; Psalm 134:2
- I kneel to honor you Almighty God; Psalm 95:6
- Guide my feet; Proverbs 4:26

Then say, "I follow God from my head to my toes!"

Wrap-Up

Prayer is communicating and building a relationship with God.

What Is Worship?

Week 2

Family Beatitude: Happy is the family who worships God, for God will empower them.

Focus: Worship

Weekly Bible Verse: *Honor the LORD for the glory of his name. Worship the LORD in the splendor of his holiness.* Psalm 29:2

Activity Options

- [ ] Worship honors God for being great. List all the words that describe God's abilities (his attributes). Then use the list to worship God.

- [ ] Jesus is the light of the world. He wants us to be lights to reflect his greatness. In the dark, shine the light from a solar powered light or flashlight onto a mirror and see if you can send the beam to another mirror. Chat about how you serve as lights.

- [ ] Jesus said that if people did not worship him, the stones would cry out (Luke 19:40). Write words that praise God on stones and place them in a container. Pull one out before bedtime and fall asleep worshiping God with that word.

Rocks That Cry Out

2 minutes

"Look Dad! I found a pink-colored stone that looks like glass," Liam said, gleefully waving it.

Dad nodded, "That's pink quartz. You can add it to your collection."

Liam placed the stone in his pocket. "I'm glad God made so many types of rocks and little stones. It makes collecting rocks really fun."

"You bet! Did you know that the Bible calls God our rock?"

"Cool. Rocks are strong and solid. God is like that."

"Yes, son, and Jesus said that the stones could cry out to praise him."

Liam thought for a moment. "I never heard a rock talk, although rolling stones can rumble and be noisy. Is that what Jesus meant?"

Dad shook his head, "When Jesus arrived in Jerusalem on a donkey's colt, some of the religious leaders got angry because people kept yelling 'Hosanna!' and that means *God saves*. The religious leaders ordered Jesus to tell his followers to stop praising him. But Jesus said—"

Liam blurted, "If the people don't praise him, the stones will! I remember this from Sunday School."

Dad high-fived Liam. "Exactly. Also, in Romans 1:20, it states that God shows us his power and ability, through his creation. Jesus created the world with God the Father, right down to little pebbles and mountains of rocks."

"Dad, I'll say, 'Hosanna' every time I pick up a rock."

Dad chuckled. "I think God will like hearing you say that."

Bible Story Connection 3–4 minutes

Read Matthew 21:1–9. Talk about the parade for Jesus and how people worshiped him.

Chat Prompts

MORE TIME?

- *Praise the Lord; praise God our savior! For each day he carries us in his arms.* Psalm 68:19

    What loads does God carry?

- *You are worthy, O Lord our God, to receive glory and honor and power. For you created all things, and they exist because you created what you pleased.* Revelation 4:11

    Why is God worthy of worship?

- *"Worship the LORD with gladness. Come before him, singing with joy.* Psalm 100:2

    Discuss worship songs you like. Do you like the lyrics? The melody? The meaning? Sing your favorites if you have time.

Prayer Journal Options

Make a memory about what you read, did, and learned this week.

- Draw stones and write praises for God.
- Write your favorite words for God and draw designs around them.
- Write your prayer needs and prayer answers.

Family Prayer: ACTS Acrostic

Acrostics help us remember facts. Each letter represents a word about prayer. This week use ACTS to remember what to pray and say words for each of these prayer elements:

- **Adore** means *worship*, and it's a word that comes from the word *worthy*. Only God is worthy of worship. We honor God who is the greatest, and know he is in control.

- **Confess** means to admit you are guilty of sinning.
- **Thanks** means to show gratefulness.
- **Supplication** means to ask God for something.

Wrap-Up

Worship is showing respect and honor to God. We honor God by praise him for our blessings and we respect him by obeying his rules for peaceful living.

What Is Sin?

Week 3

Family Beatitude: Happy is the family who confesses their sins, for they will know the freedom of forgiveness.

Focus: Sin and forgiveness

Weekly Bible Verse: *If we confess our sins to him, he is faithful and just to forgive us our sins and to cleanse us from all wickedness.* 1 John 1:9

Activity Options

- [ ] Feel soft and hard objects. Discuss angry, unforgiving hard hearts and soft, forgiven hearts.

- [ ] How are sins like weeds? Try pulling out weeds in a garden. Water the garden and then gently tug on the weeds. They come up easier. Compare how the living water of the Holy Spirit waters our hearts and makes it easier to remove sins.

- [ ] Wash off dirt from hands. Discuss how forgiveness washes your heart.

Weeding 2 minutes

Jessica started tugging on weeds to pull them out. "This is hard work," she said. She kept tugging.

Daddy turned on the hose and watered the garden. He sprinkled water on Jessica.

She giggled. "That feels so cool and good. You washed away the dirt."

Daddy said, "Water helps in many ways. Try pulling weeds now."

One yank and a weed popped out of the dirt. Jessica said, "It's easier."

Dad replied, "The water loosens the dirt so it's easier to pull a weed. It's also muddy and it's good you are wearing gloves. I can see the flowers and plants better now."

"It looks better." Jessica was quiet for a moment. "But why did I have to weed for disobeying? I said I was sorry."

"It's a good way for us to talk about sin. Disobeying is a sin. We want your heart to be beautiful like a well weeded garden."

Jessica said, "The flowers look prettier when weeds don't hide them."

"Yes. And if sin stays in your heart, it's like letting weeds grow up that will choke out good plants. Forgiveness pulls out those heart weeds. The water loosens the dirt like the Holy Spirit and God's love loosens the sin and helps you be sorry for sins."

Jessica nodded and said, "I want a good heart."

Bible Story Connection 3–4 minutes

Read Luke 22:31–34 and 47–62. Discuss how Jesus knew Peter would sin and how Peter would feel.

Chat Prompts

- *If you forgive those who sin against you, your heavenly Father will forgive you.* Matthew 6:14

    Discuss forgiveness. If you feel comfortable, share a time when it was hard to forgive someone. Why was it hard? What did you expect the other person to say when you said that you forgave them?

MORE TIME?

- *All wicked actions are sin, but not every sin leads to death.* 1 John 5:17

    Chat about sin and disobedience. Is it easier to sin or to avoid sin? Why? Which of the Ten Commandments do you think warns against the worst sin? Why?

- *For this is how God loved the world: He gave his one and only Son, so that everyone who believes in him will not perish but have eternal life.* John 3:16

    Talk about believing in God and his Son. Ask each family member to share how they accepted Jesus as their Savior. If some have not, ask them to share why.

Prayer Journal Options

Make a memory about what you read, did, and learned this week.

- Draw a cross. Write what you believe.
- Draw weeds. List some sins God has forgiven you for.
- Draw a heart. Write about God's love and forgiveness.

Family Prayer: A-B-C Prayer

It's important to believe in Jesus because he forgives us of our sins. Read Acts 16:31. Use a simple A-B-C prayer to help children understand.

- *A* is for me to admit I sin. I am thankful that Jesus died for me and forgives my sins.
- *B* is for believe. I believe in God, the Father, God the Son Jesus, and God the Holy Spirit. Jesus is the way to Heaven.
- *C* is for confess and commit. I am sorry for my sins. As I learned in Acts 16:31, I am saved because I believe in the Lord Jesus Christ. I give my life to you Lord.

Wrap-Up

Sin is breaking God's rules. It's important to forgive others when they sin against you because then God will forgive you for your sins.

What Does God Do for Me?

Week 4

Family Beatitude: Happy is the family with grateful hearts, for they will be cheerful.

Focus: Giving thanks to God

Weekly Bible Verse: *Devote yourselves to prayer with an alert mind and a thankful heart.* Colossians 4:2

Activity Options

- ☐ Make rainbow rocks: Mix 2 cups of baking soda with 1 tablespoon water in a bowl until it feels like damp sand (add 1 teaspoon more water at a time if needed). Form seven little balls from the mixture. Line them up on parchment paper. Drop food coloring onto each ball for each color in the rainbow in order (ROYGBIV). Freeze for at least 2 hours. Set the balls on a large dish and pour vinegar on each ball. Watch the bubbles and colors erupt and swirl. Talk about the promise God made with the first rainbow (Genesis 9:12–13).

- ☐ Review your prayer journal and thank God for answered prayers.

- ☐ At night, spend a few minutes thanking God while getting tucked into bed.

Family Devotion — Read Aloud

The Terrible Day 2 minutes

"How was everyone's day?" Dad asked after the dinner prayer. Everyone groaned.

"This is the second dinner I made because I burned the first one," Mom grumbled.

"I struck out every time at bat, blanked out on a test, and tore my shirt," Bobby complained.

"I forgot my homework and lunch. Also I drove my bike through a puddle on the way to school and kids laughed at my dirty clothes," Anika whined. "Plus, the dog chewed my favorite pillow. What about you, Dad?"

Dad sighed, "My boss rejected my new proposal, so I have to start over, and cars kept cutting in from of me on the drive home." An awkward silence settled over the room.

Suddenly, Bobby perked up. "I know we all had a rough day, but we can thank God for our day since we are safe, and God made this day."

Before anyone could react, the doorbell rang. Everyone froze. Was it possible that more bad news was lurking behind the door? Mom answered it. Everyone leaned from their chairs to get a good look.

"Surprise!" A neighbor stood there with a big tray of cookies. She said, "I decided to bake today and made extras for your family. I felt like God wanted me to bless you."

Everyone yelled out, "Hooray!"

Dad said, "God knew we needed a blessing."

Bible Story Connection 3–4 minutes

Read about the rainbow and Noah after the terrible flood, in Genesis 9:8–17. Discuss how God's rainbow reminds us that God cares about us and how we should care about following God.

Chat Prompts

- *I will praise you, L*ORD*, with all my heart; I will tell of all the marvelous things you have done.* Psalm 9:1

    Discuss how sharing answers to prayers gives people hope.

- *Enter his gates with thanksgiving; go into his courts with praise. Give thanks to him and praise his name.* Psalm 100:4

    Your church may not have gates or courtyards, but you can still praise God on your way to church. Maybe you can put on worship music in the car ride or discuss things you are thankful for as a family. Chat about thanking God before going to church.

- *Give thanks to the L*ORD *and proclaim his greatness. Let the whole world know what he has done.* Psalm 105:1

    What are some things that are great about God? Talk about God's love and goodness.

MORE TIME?

Prayer Journal Options

Make a memory about what you read, did, and learned this week.

- Draw a rainbow and list prayer answers.
- Draw a pillow and list blessings as a reminder that you can take comfort in God's promises.
- Write prayer requests and thank God for answers he will send.

Family Prayer: Overflowing Cup of Thanks

Gather a large cup, bowl, two regular cups, water, red and blue food coloring, and 1/8 measuring cup (or small scoop).

1. Put a large empty cup inside an empty bowl. Fill two other cups with water.
2. Drop a little red food coloring into one cup of water and blue into the other. **Our hopes (blue) and God's blood (red) mixed together make a royal color.**
3. Take turns filling the 1/8 measuring cup with colored water, alternating between blue and red, and pour it into the large cup in the bowl. Voice your hopes for the future as you add the blue water.
4. Continue until the water overflows the cup. Chat about how thanks for little and big blessings fills our hearts to overflow with joy.

Wrap-Up

Whenever you have a negative thought this week, pause. Try to focus on a blessing instead and be thankful for all the blessings God has given.

Does It Help to Pray for Other People?

Week 5

Family Beatitude: Happy is the family who prays for others, for they will be prayer warriors.

Focus: Praying for others

Weekly Bible Verse: *Keep on asking, and you will receive what you ask for. Keep on seeking, and you will find. Keep on knocking, and the door will be opened to you.* Matthew 7:7

Activity Options

- ☐ Use a globe or world map. Close your eyes and point to a place. Look up the place, find out about the people there, and pray for them.

- ☐ Make a card, wrap a little gift, or make a treat and deliver it to someone to bless them. Pray for the person while making it.

- ☐ Discuss good manners and what good prayer manners should include like saying hello, thanks, and goodbye to God.

FAMILY DEVOTION • READ ALOUD

Prayer Warriors 2 minutes

"Are you soldiers for God?" Mom asked, pointing to the children's tinfoil helmets and breastplates.

"Does God need soldiers?" Cameron asked.

"Yes. He needs us to use the strongest weapon, the power of prayer."

Chelsea asked, "What? How is prayer a weapon? We pray at meals for food and bedtime for our family."

Mom said, "I pray every day for people who need healing or help with problems. They are people I know from church, online friends, and family, or people in the news."

"Does it help?" asked Cameron.

Mom nodded. "Yes. Your dad went to the hospital last week to pray with other men from church for a friend who was sick, and doctors could not lower his fever. As they prayed, the man's fever went away. The man is back home now."

"Oh, that prayer killed germs and healed him." Cameron said.

Chelsea said, "So God can show us who needs prayer?"

"God can put a name in our thoughts." Mom explained, "Or someone might ask for prayer or share a need."

"I'm ready to be a prayer warrior," Cameron declared eagerly.

Bible Story Connection 3–4 minutes

Read about friends who asked Jesus to help their sick friend in Mark 2:1–12.

Chat Prompts

- *You can ask for anything in my name, and I will do it, so that the Son can bring glory to the Father.* John 14:13

    God loves to listen to his children's prayers and to answer them. This doesn't mean that if you ask for money it will appear. How do the week's verse and this Scripture remind us Jesus answers prayers?

MORE TIME?

- *[Isaiah] heard the Lord asking, "Whom should I send as a messenger to this people? Who will go for us?" [Isaiah] said, "Here I am. Send me."* Isaiah 6:8

    God needed to send a prophet to his people, the Jews. He asked who was willing to go and Isaiah volunteered. He prayed so often that he knew God's voice and recognized the calling. Discuss how God wants you to pray for others.

- *Ask me and I will tell you remarkable secrets you do not know about things to come.* Jeremiah 33:3

    God knows everything that will happen before it happens. Discuss how God enlightens us when we pray for wisdom.

Prayer Journal Options

Make a memory about what you read, did, and learned this week.

- Draw a heart and name some people you pray for often.
- Draw a globe and write the place you pointed. Look up facts about the country and pray for people there.
- List prayer manners.

Family Prayer: Sphere of Influence

1. Draw or print a map of the world, USA, or your state depending on how spread out your family lives.
2. Use a red heart to show where you live.
3. Draw brown dots where family members live.
4. Draw green dots of homes of friends who live far away.
5. Draw purple dots at places you visited.
6. Draw lines from the heart to the dots (using colors of the dots).

Notice how far your influence goes. Each day this week pray for all the people of one of the colors of dots.

Wrap-Up

Be a prayer warrior by praying for family, friends, enemies, and strangers.

How Did Jesus Pray?

Week 6

Family Beatitude: Happy is the family that learns to pray like Jesus taught, for they will understand how to talk to God.

Focus: Praying as Jesus taught

Weekly Bible Verse: *Pray like this: Our Father in heaven, may your name be kept holy.* Matthew 6:9

Activity Options

- [ ] Learn the first part of the Lord's Prayer, also called The Our Father. Read Matthew 6:9–10.
- [ ] Make crowns and talk about Heaven.
- [ ] Turn on a light switch and other items connected to electricity. Chat about how prayer connects us to God and God's power.
- [ ] Names matter, so we should never call people names that hurt. Draw your name down a paper. Write a word next to each letter to describe you. Do this with the name Christ and words to describe Jesus.

Barefoot Fun 2 minutes

Auntie Brooke, Sarah, and Tyler took off their shoes and socks and ran barefoot in the grass.

Sarah said, "The grass is so green and soft."

"Yes," Auntie Brooke said. "Let's thank God for that."

"Should we put our shoes on if we're going to pray?" Tyler asked.

"You don't have to," Sarah said, "Remember our Sunday school lesson? When Moses stood in front of the Burning Bush and God told Moses to take off his shoes?"

Tyler nodded, "Right, because he stood on holy ground since God was with him."

Sarah asked, "Can we run and jump too? I feel so happy and free. The breeze is blowing on my face."

Auntie Brooke laughed and said, "God likes us to be happy so let's do it. We can call out a praise or name for God and then jump and run as we repeat it."

Sarah yelled, "My God is awesome."

Everyone ran and yelled, "God is awesome!" They ran around in a circle shouting praises and repeating them. When they got tired, they dropped on the grass and giggled.

Auntie Brooke said, "God is holy. Sometimes we need to kneel and honor God quietly. That's being reverent." They knelt and whispered names for God.

Bible Story Connection 3–4 minutes

Read Exodus 3:1–14 when Moses discovered the Burning Bush and God said his name. Praise God barefoot!

Chat Prompts

- *Seek the Kingdom of God above all else, and live righteously, and he will give you everything you need.* Matthew 6:33

    Heaven is sometimes described as the Kingdom of God. It is a holy place. How do you imagine Heaven to look, feel, smell, or sound?

- *Commit your actions to the LORD, and your plans will succeed.* Proverbs 16:3

    Committing your actions to God means that you make an effort to act in a way that will please God. What type of actions please God? Discuss letting God be the leader in your actions.

- *At the name of Jesus every knee should bow, in heaven and on earth and under the earth.* Philippians 2:10

    Look up the meaning of the name "Jesus." How does the meaning relate to Jesus' sacrifice on the cross? Chat about the importance of the name Jesus.

MORE TIME?

Prayer Journal Options

Make a memory about what you read, did, and learned this week.

- Draw a crown and write words for God.
- Draw feet and write about being barefoot.
- Write prayer answers and blessings.

Family Prayer: Honor God with Praise

As you begin to pray, greet God as Jesus started the Lord's Prayer. Jesus called God *Abba* and that means father or daddy. Find names for God online or in a cyclopedic index. Say the name and praise God for who he is. Here are a few:

Wrap-Up

Follow the Lord's Prayer to pray like Jesus. Remember God's names are holy

Name	Meaning	Similar Words	Reference
Yahweh	The Lord God will Provide	Provider	Genesis 22:8
Elohim	God, Judge, Creator	Creator	Genesis 1:1–2
Adonai	Master over all	Lord	Deuteronomy 3:24
El Elyon	Most High God	Exalted, Sovereign	Genesis 14:18
El Shaddai	Lord God Almighty	Almighty, Mighty God	Genesis 17:1

What Is Daily Bread?

Week 7

Family Beatitude: Happy is the family who prays to God Our Father for they know they are God's children.

Focus: Understanding the second part of the Lord's Prayer

Weekly Bible Verse: *Don't copy the behavior and customs of this world, but let God transform you into a new person by changing the way you think. Then you will learn to know God's will for you, which is good and pleasing and perfect.* Romans 12:2

Activity Options

- [ ] Bake bread as a family and discuss daily bread.

- [ ] Set up an obstacle course and get creative. Try to do it blindfolded. Try it as a three-legged race. Time it and see who can complete it the fastest. Chat about temptation as obstacles in our relationship with God.

- [ ] Light a candle. Watch the glow and discuss the glory of God in Isaiah 60:19.

Agape Meal 2 minutes

"A grape meal?" Aurora read the weekly food calendar on the fridge. She turned to her brother, "What's a grape meal?"

"It says, *Agape*." Jordan corrected.

"Well, that still doesn't make sense," said Aurora.

Just then, their step-dad Mark called them to the dinner table. He sat beside their mom and on the table there was a loaf of bread and a bowl of grapes.

Aurora had a funny feeling. "Is this a snack or a lesson?"

Mom laughed. "It's a special fellowship time," she said as the kids sat down. Mark passed out the bread and grapes as mom continued. "The first believers in Jesus met for meals that called agape meals. *Agape* means love."

Mark smiled, "As we share bread and grapes, we want to talk about God's love, thank God for bread, and remember how Jesus broke bread."

Jordan said, "Like when he fed the crowds and ate with his friends the night before he died."

"Is that why we pray give us this day our daily bread?" Aurora asked.

"Yes, that's in the Lord's prayer." Mark said. "Jesus called himself the Bread of Life. Asking for daily bread is also asking for Jesus to be with us."

Mom said, "Let's pray and thank Jesus for being our bread of life."

Bible Story Connection 3–4 minutes

Read Acts 16:6–25 to understand how the Holy Spirit guided Paul to show him God's will.

Chat Prompts

- *As they were eating, Jesus took some bread and blessed it. Then he broke it in pieces and gave it to the disciples, saying, "Take it, for this is my body."* Mark 14:22

  The Last Supper was the last meal that Jesus shared with his disciples before he was arrested and crucified. During that meal he broke bread with the disciples. Why did he do this?

MORE TIME?

- *All the believers devoted themselves to the apostles' teaching, and to fellowship, and to sharing in meals (including the Lord's Supper), and to prayer.* Acts 2:42

  The first believers did not have fancy churches to pray in and worship God. Instead, they met together at friends houses and shared meals. This is called fellowship. What does fellowship mean to you?

- *People will come from all over the world—from east and west, north and south—to take their places in the Kingdom of God.* Luke 13:29

  The Kingdom of God will be filled with people from all over the world. How do you imagine God's feast in Heaven?

Prayer Journal Options

Make a memory about what you read, did, and learned this week.

- Draw bread and list some needs.
- Draw a stop sign and list temptations to avoid.

Family Prayer: Symbols for Praying

> **Wrap-Up**
> Let the Lord's Prayer guide your prayer life.

Make a Lord's Prayer booklet. From colored construction paper, cut out 3x5-inch rectangles, one for each color mentioned below. On each colored card, draw the associated symbol from the chart. When complete, staple together in order. Let the symbols and colors remind you of the meaning of the Lord's Prayer.

Color/Meaning	Symbol	Words	Why
white/pure	number 1	Our Father	1 true God
blue/God sees us	cloud with eyes	in heaven	where God lives
green/evergreen	tree	may your name be kept holy.	eternal
purple/royalty	crown	May your Kingdom come soon.	king
brown/earth	one way sign	May your will be done on earth, as it is in heaven.	God's way
yellow/grain color	bread	Give us today the food we need	provisions
silver (gray)/money	silver coin	and forgive us our sins, as we have forgiven those who sin against us.	forgiveness
black/darkness	blank	And don't let us yield to temptation,	temptation
red/blood	cross of hearts	but rescue us from the evil one.	God is love

Week 8

Does God See My Tears?

Family Beatitude: Happy is the family who shares their tears for they will be comforted.

Focus: Responding to bad news

Weekly Bible Verse: *When I heard this, I sat down and wept. In fact, for days I mourned, fasted, and prayed to the God of heaven.* Nehemiah 1:4

Activity Options

- [ ] Make a water lens with an empty plastic bucket.
    1. Cover the opening of the bucket with plastic wrap.
    2. Secure the plastic wrap with duct tape or a large rubber band.
    3. Cut two circular openings around the sides of the bucket large enough to slip your hand inside.
    4. Fill the plastic with water. It will sag to make a concave lens.
    5. Hold objects under the lens to see the water magnify the items.
    6. Discuss how tears make problems look bigger.

- [ ] Cut an onion. It will make you cry because chemicals that irritate eyes are released in the air when we cut onions.

- [ ] Care for your eyes after crying. Place a cold compress or chilled cucumber slices on your eyes.

News That Brought Tears 2 minutes

"Mom, are you OK?" Rachel asked when she entered the living room. On the couch, Dad sat with his arm around Mom. Mom's eyes were red and puffy.

"Your grandma had a stroke last night," Mom explained slowly. "Her blood stopped flowing to her brain for a while. She's alive but we don't know if she'll live or be able to walk."

Rachel hugged her mom and said, "That's terrible. I love Grandma. Can we pray?"

Mom wiped away a tear and nodded. Dad started to pray as they all held hands.

After praying, Dad's phone rang. He answered it and left the room. A few minutes later, he came back and said, "There's more bad news." Rachel felt Mom tense beside her. "Grandma had a cerebral hemorrhage. Her blood is leaking and flowing through her brain. She's in surgery now."

Both Mom and Rachel burst into tears and leaned into each other. Dad joined them on the couch. They prayed again.

Dad said, "We need to trust that God will heal Grandma, but even if he doesn't, we know that he is with us. In the Bible, a man named Nehemiah cried when he heard bad news. He started praying. He prayed for many days. After four months God answered his prayer."

Rachel said, "Let's read that. I want to keep praying. I won't give up trusting God for a miracle."

Bible Story Connection 3–4 minutes

Read the first chapter of Nehemiah. Chat about the news that made Nehemiah cry and what he did next.

Chat Prompts

- *You keep track of all my sorrows. You have collected all my tears in your bottle. You have recorded each one in your book.* Psalm 56:8

    Talk about emotions and how it's natural to cry when you feel sad. Discuss how God sees those tears.

MORE TIME?

- *He will wipe every tear from their eyes, and there will be no more death or sorrow or crying or pain. All these things are gone forever.* Revelation 21:4

    In Heaven, there will not be any pain or sorrow. Can you even imagine a place like that? Discuss tearless Heaven.

- *The LORD has heard my plea; the LORD will answer my prayer.* Psalm 6:9

    God hears every prayer and plea. He promises that he'll answer our prayers, but he often does it in a way that we don't expect. Can you think of a time that God answered your prayers in a surprising way? Chat about how God hears our prayers.

Prayer Journal Options

Make a memory about what you read, did, and learned this week.

- List each person's prayer needs and how God responds.
- Draw tears and describe the problem.
- Write any answers to prayer.

Family Prayer: Corn Kernel Praises

Set a bowl on the table and gather around. Divide ½ cup of unpopped kernels between all players.

Set a pan on the stove top and add two tablespoons of cooking oil. Add two unpopped kernels. Cover with lid and turn up to medium heat. Listen for the two kernels to pop.

Wrap-Up

Turn tears to prayers. Tell God why you cried and what you need.

Each person shares a praise or an answered prayer. When they finish speaking, everyone drops a kernel into the bowl. Once the two kernels in the pan have popped, everyone puts the remainder of their kernels in the bowl. Add the kernels to the pot. Watch the kernels explode out from a dry, hard kernel to a fluffy piece of corn that's good to eat. Praise helps our hearts pop with joy!

How Soon Will God Answer My Prayer?

Week 9

Family Beatitude: Happy is the family who persists in prayer, for they will see God answer.

Focus: Persistent prayer

Weekly Bible Verse: *Hannah was in deep anguish, crying bitterly as she prayed to the L ORD.* 1 Samuel 1:10

Activity Options

- ☐ Open an adhesive bandage and write some words of comfort on it like *God loves you* or *believe*. Place it over your heart as a reminder God heals our heart hurts.

- ☐ Ride a rollercoaster or drive up and down a hilly area. Chat about the downs of challenges and the ups of prayer answers.

- ☐ Consider various reaction times such as how long it takes to bake bread or see bubbles form after pouring vinegar onto baking soda. The process and ingredients impact the timing. Chat about God's timing in answering prayers.

Roller Coaster Prayers 2 minutes

Rachel arrived home and asked, "How's Grandma?"

Her mom said, "She came through the surgery. We must pray and wait."

For weeks Rachel, her step-brother Matthew, and their family prayed. Grandma had a second hemorrhage and more surgeries.

Matthew said, "It's like riding a prayer rollercoaster."

At last Grandma transferred to a rehabilitation center. For months they prayed that God would heal Grandma completely. They wanted to see her, but she lived far away.

Almost two years later, Grandma and Grandpa came to visit for a few months. Hooray! Grandma walked with a walker, but she was strong enough to swim with them in the pool.

Rachel hugged her and said, "I love you. I learned to do manicures. Can I do your nails?" Grandma nodded.

Rachel painted her grandma's nails weekly and sometimes added sparkles or little nail stickers.

Matthew played games with Grandma, and they all enjoyed sharing jokes. They thanked God for healing Grandma.

Bible Story Connection 3–4 minutes

Read 1 Samuel 1:6–20 and learn about Hannah's persistent prayer to have a child. Chat about how she cried before God answered her prayer.

Chat Prompts

- *Dear brothers and sisters, when troubles of any kind come your way, consider it an opportunity for great joy. For you know that when your faith is tested, your endurance has a chance to grow.* James 1:2–3

    Few people look forward to problems or trials, but these verses tell us to rejoice! It is during these times that we are reminded to rely on God and not ourselves. Chat about how there are many problems in our lives and each one is an opportunity to pray.

MORE TIME?

- *Rejoice in our confident hope. Be patient in trouble, and keep on praying.* Romans 12:12

    Talk about being persistent. How can we keep praying when we get tired of waiting?

- *Wait patiently for the LORD. Be brave and courageous. Yes, wait patiently for the LORD.* Psalm 27:14

    When a Bible verse repeats the same phrase, you should pay extra attention because it's extra important. Waiting patiently is hard work, so this verse encourages us to be brave and courageous. How can praise help you wait for God to answer a prayer?

Prayer Journal Options

Make a memory about what you read, did, and learned this week.

- Draw a rollercoaster and write about praying when things go up and down.
- Check last week's prayers and record any progress or praises.
- List unanswered prayers to keep praying and trusting God to answer.

Family Prayer: Prayer Chart

Starting from left to right, use a word from each column of the prayer chart to form a prayer. For example: Almighty God, your child (say your name) praises you for friends like (say names and why you're thankful for them). In Jesus' name, amen.

Add your own words or make your own chart.

Wrap-Up

No one knows how long it takes God to answer prayers, but be persistent. Keep praying when God does not answer right away.

Name for God	Name for You	Action	Object (Prayer Need)
Almighty God	Child	Praises	Friends
Dear Daddy	Grateful Kid	Needs	Blessings
Savior	Saved	Help Needed	Family
Holy Spirit	Beloved	Sorry	Health
Creator	Lamb	Forgive	School

How Can I Praise God?

Week 10

Family Beatitude: Happy is the family that blows kisses and hugs to God, for they will laugh and rejoice.

Focus: Praise

Weekly Bible Verse: *Each morning and evening they stood before the LORD to sing songs of thanks and praise to him.* 1 Chronicles 23:30

Activity Options

- [ ] Sing and praise God with music you make or play. Have a praise parade or move around.
- [ ] Every morning let everyone praise God for a blessing he sent.
- [ ] Write prayer answers on a chalk- or whiteboard so everyone can praise God for the answer.

Brand-New Day! 2 minutes

Rebecca opened the drapes in her mom's room and yelled, "Mom it's a brand-new day! The sun is shining."

Her mom opened her eyes and sighed. She said, "I think it came early today."

Rebecca giggled and said, "It's play day at the park. I'm so happy that I wish I could hug God."

Mom laughed. "Well, before you try, let's get ready for the day."

After breakfast, they headed to the park. She wanted to try giving God a hug. She crossed her arms and said, "This is a big hug." Then, she opened her arms wide and looked up to the sky and said, "I'm sending the hug to you, God."

Next, they kept their arms open wide and praised God, "You are great. You made the blue sky and the sunshine. You love me." Then they pulled their arms down and wrapped them around their shoulders in another hug. Mom said, "Now that's a hug from God."

Rebecca's mom opened a bottle of bubbles. As they continued praising God, after each praise, they blew a kiss to God by blowing bubbles.

Bible Story Connection 3–4 minutes

Read Lamentations 3:19–25. Discuss how even though we have problems we know every morning that it's a new day and we have new reasons to be thankful and trust God.

Chat Prompt

- *The wind blows wherever it wants. Just as you can hear the wind but can't tell where it comes from or where it is going, so you can't explain how people are born of the Spirit.* John 3:8

    Discuss the wind and God's presence. Chat about praising God and blowing kisses to God.

- *Arise, Jerusalem! Let your light shine for all to see. For the glory of the LORD rises to shine on you.* Isaiah 60:1

    Discuss how sunlight reminds us how God shines light into our world and our hearts.

- *This is the LORD's doing, and it is wonderful to see.* Psalm 118:23

    Sometimes, something comes together so perfectly that you realize God must have organized it. Whether it was meeting a new friend in a time of need or being in the right place at the right time, God can use anything to accomplish his plans. Chat about thanking God every morning for the new day and new opportunities.

MORE TIME?

Prayer Journal Options

Make a memory about what you read, did, and learned this week.

- Draw bubbles and write any new praises inside.
- Write today's blessings.
- Draw kisses going to Heaven.

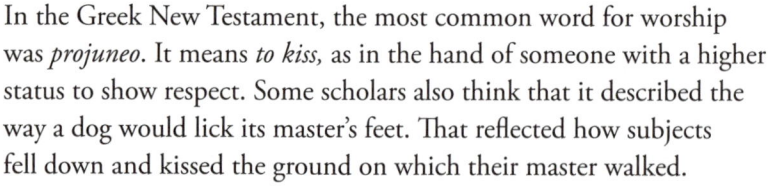

Family Prayer: Praise God with Hugs

In the Greek New Testament, the most common word for worship was *projuneo*. It means *to kiss,* as in the hand of someone with a higher status to show respect. Some scholars also think that it described the way a dog would lick its master's feet. That reflected how subjects fell down and kissed the ground on which their master walked.

When we worship God, we show him respect and honor. Today, show God how much you love him. Say a praise into your hand and then blow a kiss up into the sky to send it to God. Keep praising God with kisses.

Wrap-Up

Praise God every day! Brainstorm creative ways to make praise a daily habit. Some ideas are enjoying God's creation, starting your day with praise songs, and keeping a grateful attitude.

What Happens When I Pray with My Family?

Week 11

Family Beatitude: Happy is the family who prays together, for God will hear them.

Focus: Praying together

Weekly Bible Verse: *I also tell you this: If two of you agree here on earth concerning anything you ask, my Father in heaven will do it for you.* Matthew 18:19

Activity Options

☐ Watch the movie *War Room* and chat about family prayer.

☐ Have a battle cry for prayer. Let it be a special sound to call family members to prayer. This might be special words to yell out, a whistle, or other noise.

☐ Make a wooden or cardboard sword to hang in the war room area. Write on it "God's Word."

Book Bag Theft 2 minutes

Kyle yelled, "Meet in the war room!"

Everyone rushed to a corner of the family room.

Kyle said, "Someone broke into the van and stole my backpack during youth group. I've lost my history book, calculator, and laptop."

Dad prayed for God to supply the missing items and forgive the thief. Kyle prayed for safe parking at church. Everyone prayed.

The next day while shopping, Michael yelled, "Look Mom! There's a backpack in the free bin, and other things Kyle needs." They grabbed the items.

Kyle found a used laptop online, but not the book.

Michael said, "I'll give you a book."

Kyle tousled his brother's hair and said, "Thanks, little bro, but I need the stolen one."

Michael replied, "We prayed in the war room. God will find it."

The next week Kyle returned from youth group and held up a book. "Look! My friend Jake found it behind the bushes of the church parking lot. I guess the thief doesn't like to study!"

Bible Story Connection 3–4 minutes

Read Acts 12:5–19. Discuss what happened when people prayed for Peter.

Chat Prompts

- *God looks down from heaven on the entire human race; he looks to see if anyone is truly wise, if anyone seeks God.* Psalm 53:2

    God is always watching over us.
    What does this verse say that he is looking for? How does someone become wise? What does it mean to seek God? Discuss what God sees when your family prays.

MORE TIME?

- *We know that God causes everything to work together for the good of those who love God and are called according to his purpose for them.* Romans 8:28

    We might think that we are in charge of our own lives, but really it's God who is in control. This verse reminds us that God is constantly working "for the good of those who love" him. Chat about how God works things out.

- *When [Peter] realized [God had sent an angel to free him], he went to the home of Mary, the mother of John Mark, where many were gathered for prayer.* Acts 12:12

    Peter visited the people who prayed from him while he was in prison. He explained how God sent an angel to free him. How do you let your prayer partners know what happened when they prayed for you?

Prayer Journal Options

Make a memory about what you read, did, and learned this week.

- Draw your prayer war room. Write or draw about answered prayers.
- Draw a circle of hands and write about what it's like to pray as a family.
- Add new prayer answers and needs.

Family Prayer: War Room Prayers

A war room is a place to gather together to pray for each other. Here are some ideas for how to create a place to pray together:

- Put pillows on the floor and sit in a circle or sit at a table with chairs.
- Hang a chalkboard to write prayer needs and praises.
- Use strategy. Post the words of David when he fought Goliath, from 1 Samuel 17:45–47 and read them. Or read Psalms that speak about battles, such as Psalm 20 and Psalm 44.

Wrap-Up

Praying with your family will give you spiritual strength. When you have a big prayer need, call your family together to pray.

For each request, pray boldly for God to give you victory.

How Do I Bless Someone?

Week 12

Family Beatitude: Happy is the family who blesses others, for they will please God.

Focus: Blessing others

Weekly Bible Verse: *Then [Jesus] took the children in his arms and placed his hands on their heads and blessed them.* Mark 10:16

Activity Options

- [ ] The Hebrew word for bless is *baruch* (BUH-rook). It's related to the word *berech* (BEH-rek) which means knee. When you "take a knee" or kneel before God you are in a position to accept a blessing. Children kneel while parents pray a blessing over each one.

- [ ] Give secret blessings. Try to bless someone with an act of kindness without the person seeing you. Make the bed, do someone's chore, or show special kindness.

- [ ] Fold a piece of paper in half. Trace your hand on folded paper with the little finger or thumb along the fold (don't cut this part!). Cut out. It's a blessing reminder card. Write ways to bless people on the card.

FAMILY DEVOTION — READ ALOUD

Bless Your Brother! 2 minutes

For evening devotions, Paul talked with his children about blessing other people. His youngest son Ethan asked, "Dad, what's a blessing and how can I bless someone?"

"A blessing is an undeserved gift, like giving a kind word to someone who looks unhappy, or giving a surprise kindness to someone sick—like when we raked leaves for Mrs. Parker. God also wants us to bless people who have been unkind to us."

Ethan thought about it, "So would it be like smiling at someone after they teased me? That would be hard."

Paul nodded. "Yes, but God wants us to love people even when they hurt us. Try to remember that God loves them as much as he loves you."

"I'll try," Ethan said with a shrug. He wasn't sure this was going to work.

The next day Ethan had a fight with his big brother Landon. Ethan stormed away, angry. Suddenly, he remembered his dad's words, "Be a blessing."

A moment later, Ethan walked back. "Hey, Landon. Do you want to play my new video game with me?"

Landon squinted and asked, "What's the catch?"

"No catch. I just thought I'd do something nice."

Suddenly, Landon remembered, too. "Oh! You're being a blessing." He laughed. "Yeah. Let's play. And . . . I'm sorry we fought."

"Me, too," Ethan said, smiling.

Bible Story Connection 3–4 minutes

Read Genesis 49:1–28 and chat about how Jacob gave each son a unique blessing.

Chat Prompts

- *May the LORD bless you and protect you.* Numbers 6:24

    Discuss how God cares for us and blesses us. Look around the room right now. How has he blessed you physically? Think of your church community. How has he blessed you spiritually?

MORE TIME?

- [God said,] *I will make you into a great nation. I will bless you and make you famous, and you will be a blessing to others.* Genesis 12:2

    God blessed Abraham because he was a faithful follower and blessed others. Chat about how God blesses us and then wants us to bless others.

- *I urge you, first of all, to pray for all people. Ask God to help them; intercede on their behalf, and give thanks for them.* 1 Timothy 2:1

    Paul told Timothy that the way to begin worship is to pray for others. To bless someone is to do something good. It can be a simple smile, encouraging word, or act of kindness. How can you bless others?

Prayer Journal Options

Make a memory about what you read, did, and learned this week.

- Draw a smiley face and write about how smiles lift spirits.
- Draw a hand and lists way to bless family members.
- Draw a larger hand and thank God for blessings.

Family Prayer: Pow Wow

The words POW and WOW make a POWerful acrostic!

Pray	**W**orship
Over	**O**ver
Worries	**W**onders

Sit in a circle. Let each person state one prayer need (worry) and one praise (wonder). Take turns praying one sentence for the worry and one sentence of praise for the wonder for the person on your right. Continue until everyone has prayed.

Praying for someone is a way to bless the person.

Wrap-Up

This chapter covered many ways that you can bless someone like offering a prayer or a helping hand. This week, make a special effort to bless someone!

When Should I Pray for Someone Else?

Week 13

Family Beatitude: Happy is the family who notices needs, for they will develop compassion.

Focus: Spotting prayer needs

Weekly Bible Verse: [Jesus said,] *"I feel sorry for these people. They have been here with me for three days, and they have nothing left to eat."* Mark 8:2

Activity Options

- ☐ Play eye spy. Include spying people who are not smiling, anyone who might need help, and also creatures who might need help.

- ☐ Prepare to give spiritual first aid. It should contain comforting and encouraging words, smiles, hugs, prayer, and a few Scripture passages.

- ☐ Make bandage notes to send or give. Decorate and stick a bandage on a card and write a prayer for healing or overcoming problems.

Daddy Ow-ee 2 minutes

Mamaw had spent a few days at Laurie's house while Mommy and Daddy went to the hospital. When they returned, Daddy's head was wrapped in a bandage and he walked with a cane. Laurie said, "Daddy has ow-ee. Mommy, did you hurt Daddy?"

Mom laughed, "No, sweetie. Daddy had something inside his head that was hurting him and gave him problems. The doctors had to make a cut and take it out."

"Ow-ee! Did they cut his leg, too?" Laurie pointed to the cane.

"No, it just helps Daddy walk while his head heals," Mom explained as she helped Daddy into his comfy seat. Laurie kissed his hand and said, "Sorry, Daddy. Hope you feel better."

Daddy smiled, "Princess, you always make me feel happy."

Laurie smiled and whispered something to Mamaw, who went to the kitchen.

Mamaw returned, giving Laurie half a glass of water that she slowly carried to Daddy. She handed it to Daddy and he drank it.

Laurie turned to Mom and said, "I spied Daddy's ow-ee. I helped. Now we pray."

Mom nodded, "Yes, you are a great prayer warrior. You spied a need, helped, and now we'll pray."

Laurie, Mom, and Mamaw held hands and prayed for Daddy.

Bible Story Connection 3–4 minutes

Read how Jesus spotted a very sad woman and helped her in Luke 7:11–17.

Chat Prompts

MORE TIME?

- *Don't look out only for your own interests, but take an interest in others, too.* Philippians 2:4

    "Spying the needs of others" means that you pay attention to what others need. How can you spy the needs of others when someone is sad? Angry? Tired? Annoyed? Disappointed?

- *If someone has enough money to live well and sees a brother or sister in need but shows no compassion— how can God's love be in that person?* 1 John 3:17

    As a kid, you might not have a lot of money. But do you have a lot of toys, books, clothes, or lunch snacks? Can you think of anyone to whom you could show compassion by sharing what you have? Share a time you noticed someone in need.

- *For we are God's masterpiece. He has created us anew in Christ Jesus, so we can do the good things he planned for us long ago.* Ephesians 2:10

    This is some really good news. As believers in Jesus, God uses us to bless other people. Discuss how you may be the answer to someone's prayer.

Prayer Journal Options

Make a memory about what you read, did, and learned this week.

- Draw eyes and list what to look for when you see people.
- Draw ears to remember to ask how someone is really doing.
- List ways to help people.

Family Prayer: Suit Up

Read Ephesians 6:10–19 and ask God to help you suit up as a warrior to defend and help others. Discuss each warrior item and how it helps. For example, a spiritual helmet protects our mind.

Pray each morning for God to show you someone to bless. At night, pray for people you blessed. Ask God to help you defeat any enemies.

Wrap-Up

You can pray for anyone at any time. Watch for people in need. If you have something that could help them, be quick to share it. It can be as simple as sharing a lunch with someone who doesn't have one.

Why Does God Let People Do Bad Things?

Week 14

Family Beatitude: Happy is the family who knows God supplies our needs, for they will be content.

Focus: God's provisions

Weekly Bible Verse: *The L<small>ORD</small> is my shepherd; I have all that I need.* Psalm 23:1

Activity Options

- ☐ Fill a water balloon with water until it pops. Chat about how anger can fill a person's heart until that person explodes. Then the anger spills out and hurts others.

- ☐ Write a list of wants. Now, next to each item, write the name of something for which you are thankful.

- ☐ Listen to some advertisements. What words imply someone deserves it or needs it? Is it true?

69

Stolen Bicycle 2 minutes

James bounded outside to ride his beautiful new three-speed bicycle. Suddenly, he stopped short. The lock on the bike rack was broken and the bicycle was gone! James hurried back inside to tell his stepmom Annie. She reported the theft; but days later, the bike was still not found.

James's dad and Annie mentioned it to their friends. Two people came by to give James a used bicycle. One had ten speeds! It was painted it green and there was a brand-new lock.

"Thank you so much!" James exclaimed when he saw it. James rode the bike on the trail and timed his ride. "Whoa, five minutes faster than my old bike!" He marveled.

At dinner that night, James shared his excitement about the bike. His dad said, "That's great, James! What are some reasons to be thankful for this bike?"

James didn't even have to think about it. He was brimming with gratitude. "We have kind friends," he said. "This is the fastest bike I've owned. A friend visiting me can ride the extra bike. It has a really comfortable seat. I had great birthday and enjoyed the other bike for a while."

Dad hugged James and said, "Great thoughts. God loves you and loves a grateful heart. That's more important than something new that will become old someday."

"I'm still praying for the thief, too. I hope that God will change his heart."

"That's great. We may never know what happens, but God will know."

Bible Story Connection 3–4 minutes

Read 1 Kings 3:1–15 and discuss the King's request. What did God offer him? What did he ask for instead of wealth or other selfish desires?

Chat Prompts

MORE TIME?

- *Not that I was ever in need, for I have learned how to be content with whatever I have.* Philippians 4:11

    How does gratitude help you be content?
    How does it change your perspective?

- *For everyone has sinned; we all fall short of God's glorious standard.* Romans 3:23

    No one can live up to God's perfect standard because we have all sinned. Thankfully, we can focus on God's forgiveness.

- [Jesus said,] *"Love your enemies! Pray for those who persecute you!"* Matthew 5:44

    It can be really hard to care about someone who has hurt you. How does forgiveness help you feel better? How can it help the person who hurt you?

Prayer Journal Options

Make a memory about what you read, did, and learned this week.

- Write an acrostic about God's love using the word *love*.
- Draw a bandage. Write about how people choose to sin and hurt others, but we can pray for and forgive them.
- List reasons to thank God today.

Family Prayer: Love Your Enemies

God does not want us to hurt other people, but he gave us freedom to make our own choices. Sadly, some people choose to hurt others. Here are some ways to treat others as God commanded:

- Forgive and pray for people who hurt you. Ask God to change them.
- Make a decision to choose to help and not hurt others.
- Replace negative thoughts (anger, revenge, complaints, etc.) and selfish desires with gratitude for what you have (love, family, health, home, etc.). Focus on being happy with what God provided. It reframes your thoughts!

Wrap-Up

God gives us a choice in everything that we do. We can choose to follow his rules and accept his blessings, or we can choose to live by our own desires. Sadly, living selfishly often hurts others. Pray for your enemies.

How Strong Is God?

Week 15

Family Beatitude: Happy is the family who knows God is strong, for he will be their prayer tower.

Focus: Pray to a strong God

Weekly Bible Verse: *You are my safe refuge, a fortress where my enemies cannot reach me.* Psalm 61:3

Activity Options

- ☐ Take a hike or go to a high place with a view. Watch what's happening below. God looks out on us like someone in a high place. Discuss the advantages of seeing things from this perspective.

- ☐ Build two towers, one with blocks and one with cards. Which one is stronger? Why?

- ☐ Pack an egg with tissue or packing materials inside a small box. Drop it from a high place. Talk about how prayers cushions us from difficult consequences.

The Tree House 2 minutes

Alex and Martin were so excited. They had spent the last week traveling with Dad to different hardware stores, lumber yards, and yard sales, to gather supplies for building their tree house. In the backyard, they organized everything they had gathered: a ladder, wood, nails, hammers, measuring tape, and a saw.

"Before we start, we should pray," Martin suggested. Dad and Alex nodded. Martin prayed, "Dear God, thank you for this beautiful sunny day so we can build our tree house. Please protect us from getting hurt, and help us to have fun! In Jesus' name, amen."

They positioned the ladder against the tree and nailed a board to two high branches to start.

Alex said, "This will be a cool tree house. It's so high I can see everywhere!"

Martin said, "Yeah, bro! It's our lookout tower."

They built the floor and sawed a square opening for a trap door. They added a rope ladder to hang down for climbing up to the fort. They built it tall enough for their dad to stand inside.

Alex climbed up and exclaimed, "Wow! I love this fort."

Dad said, "High-five, boys!" They all smacked palms. "Excellent work. You know, we can read about good watch towers in the Bible and discuss good uses for this fort."

"Well, I guess that means no bombing kids with water balloons, but we could do an egg drop," Martin said.

Dad laughed and said, "Let's focus on some good uses for the fort."

Bible Story Connection 3–4 minutes

In the Old Testament, watchtowers served as lookouts to alert cities of danger. Read Nehemiah 3:1,11,25–27; 12:38–39.

There were two important Hebrew words mentioned: *Hananel (HAY-nay-nuhl)*, meaning God is gracious, and *mizpah (MIHZ-puh)*, meaning watchtower. Reread Nehemiah 12:38–39 replacing these Hebrew words with their meanings. How does this change your understanding of the verses?

> Think of each prayer to God like a brick in a tower. The more bricks, the stronger the tower becomes and the greater your faith in God grows.

Chat Prompts

- *Those who fear the L{{\sc ord}} are secure; he will be a refuge for their children.* Proverbs 14:26

    Discuss modern towers like air control towers. How is God like a tower or fort?

MORE TIME?

- *[King Uzziah] built structures on the walls of Jerusalem, designed by experts to protect those who shot arrows and hurled large stones from the towers and the corners of the wall.* 2 Chronicles 26:15

    How do our prayers serve as weapons against spiritual warfare?

- *He will cover you with his feathers. He will shelter you with his wings. His faithful promises are your armor and protection.* Psalm 91:4

    Talk about how feathers are soft but they protect birds. How does a shield protect a soldier?

Prayer Journal Options

Make a memory about what you read, did, and learned this week.

- Draw a tower. Write how you need God's protection.
- Draw a feather and shield. Ask God to shield you.
- Make an acrostic from the word weapon describing how prayer is a weapon.

Family Prayer: Prayer Towers

1. Insert a skewer into a block of foam so that it stands upright. Glue the skewer to the foam base if necessary.
2. Cut strips of paper about 3x4 inches.
3. Punch a hole in the center of each slip of paper.
4. Write prayers of thanks and prayer needs on slips of paper.
5. Slide the slips of paper on the skewer to build a tower of prayers!
6. Another day read those prayers and needs and remember how praying to a strong God brings answers.

Wrap-Up

God's power is the strongest thing ever, but we need to believe in his power to see miracles. Prayer connects us to God, who is our strong watchtower.

How Do I Know God's Will?

Week 16

Family Beatitude: Happy is the family who applies God's Word, for they will discern his will.

Focus: Knowing God's will

Weekly Bible Verse: *"For I know the plans I have for you,"* says the LORD. *"They are plans for good and not for disaster, to give you a future and a hope."* Jeremiah 29:11

Activity Option

Prepare: Glue small objects to an index card (rubber bands, coins, stickers, crayons, etc.). Place card in an envelope and seal it. Make one for each child.

- ☐ **Day 1** Children feel envelope and rub pencils over envelope to guess contents. Discuss how we discover talents as we interact with people.

- ☐ **Day 2:** Open the envelopes. Share how God can open our eyes to see gifts and his will.

- ☐ **Day 3:** Discuss how each object can be used for good or evil (i.e. rubber bands to hurt or help). Discuss free will and God's will.

Why Did I Fall? 2 minutes

Ray gathered his children in the living room and held out a large grocery tote. He said, "I've prayed for God to make this bag support me." Then he hung the bag handles over two chairs and tried to sit down on the bag like a hammock seat. *Thud!* The bag slipped off the chairs and Ray landed on the floor. Everyone laughed.

The children yelled, "You can't tell God what to do."

Ray said, "Good thoughts. The bag's purpose is to hold groceries but it's not meant to hold me. God also gave each person a purpose."

Noah asked, "How will we know God's purpose for us?"

"It's a process. The Bible helps us know how to live and understand what is right. God gave us talents and gifts. I'm great with numbers, so when God opened doors for accounting, that matched my talents. He's blessed that work."

"So, he won't just zap me like the apostle Paul or give me a vision?" Oliver asked.

"Sometimes he does." Mom chimed in. "We need to practice listening for his voice, and the voice of godly people, and to look for opportunities God provides. When the pastor asked me to teach, I believed God used the pastor to show me God's will."

"People can show us God's will?" Amelia questioned.

"Sometimes," said Mom. "I also prayed and my mind filled with ideas of how to teach. That confirmed God's will."

"God has a purpose for everyone!" Noah cheered.

Bible Story Connection 3–4 minutes

Read Mark 1:16–20. Discuss how like the disciples, God calls us to follow him. We will each have a unique path.

Chat Prompts

- *Don't just listen to God's word. You must do what it says. Otherwise, you are only fooling yourselves.* James 1:22

    Is it easy or hard to read the Bible every day? Why? Chat about how doing God's will includes obeying and applying Scriptures.

MORE TIME?

- *If you look for me wholeheartedly, you will find me.* Jeremiah 29:13

    What does it mean to do something wholeheartedly? Discuss things that you put a lot of effort into because you care about it. How God will respond when we seek God's will with our whole heart?

- *That night Paul had a vision: A man from Macedonia in northern Greece was standing there, pleading with him, "Come over to Macedonia and help us!" So we decided to leave for Macedonia at once, having concluded that God was calling us to preach the Good News there.* Acts 16:9–10

    Chat about unusual dreams, visions, or hearing God's voice. We'll recognize his voice through listening, especially when we pray.

Prayer Journal Options

Make a memory about what you read, did, and learned this week.

- Draw ducks (See below.) and list choices you need to make.
- Draw ears and write what you heard from God.
- Draw pictures that remind you of your family members' talents and gifts.

> **Wrap-Up**
>
> If you seek God with your whole heart then you will know God's will.

Family Prayer: Ducks in a Row Prayers

Buy five toy ducks or draw a picture of a duck on five separate pieces of paper. Place a word from the first column on each of the five ducks. When you have a decision to make, take one duck at a time and pray what is written on the duck. Write the date you prayed in the chart.

Word	Pray	Lined Up
Scripture		Bible verses confirm the godly choice.
Circumstances		Doors open, supplies and funds are provided, etc.
Peace		You have inner peace.
Counsel		Wise advisors agree.
Common Sense		Choice makes sense.

Line ducks on a shelf as prayers are answered. When they are all lined up, act on the decision. Watch for and record confirmations (signs of blessing).

Can God Help Me Stop Worrying?

Week 17

Family Beatitude: Happy is the family who lets go of worry, for they will have peace.

Focus: Giving cares to God

Weekly Bible Verse: *So don't worry about tomorrow, for tomorrow will bring its own worries. Today's trouble is enough for today.* Matthew 6:34

Activity Options

- ☐ Play tug-of-war. Chat about pulling back when we try to give something to God.

- ☐ Play Who's in Charge. Choose one person to be It and have them close their eyes. Silently choose a Leader for the group. It opens their eyes and stands in the center of the circle. The Leader makes motions that others follow. It tries to identify the Leader.

- ☐ Experiment with heat by melting ice cubes. Some people say that they are "on fire for God" when they are passionate about their faith. When we are on fire for God in prayer, our worries melt away.

Tug-of-War 2 minutes

"Anyone wanna play tug-of-war?" Uncle Vic asked, swinging the rope in his hand. Mickey and Jaime hurried down from the tree house and Auntie June put down her book on the lawn chair. "I'll take you all down," Uncle Vic challenged.

Auntie June got a strange gleam in her eye. "OK, you heard him. It's us three against Uncle Vic."

Everyone got into position with Uncle Vic on one side and Auntie June, Mickey, and Jaime on the other side. "One, two, three, PULL!" Jaime shouted. They pulled Uncle Vic across the line into the mud.

He laughed, "Now I'm stuck in the mud!" They took the rope and helped pull him out. Then, they all plopped onto the grass laughing.

"OK, so I don't work well as a one-man team," Uncle Vic admitted, "But I actually wanted to play this so that we could compare it to prayer."

"Does God play tug-of-war when we pray?" Mickey asked, confused.

Uncle Vic explained, "No, when we give a worry to God and then keep worrying, it's like pulling our prayer back. We try to control the answer and not let God give us his best answer."

Auntie June said, "There's a popular saying about what we should do when we have a worry: Let go and let God."

Jaime smiled. "That's what we should have done playing Tug of War. Let go and let Uncle Vic fall!"

"You'd better not!" Uncle Vic said. "Let's do it again!" Everyone laughed as they got up to try again.

Bible Story Connection 3–4 minutes

Read Matthew 17:14–21 and Mark 4:38–40. Discuss how Jesus reacted each time the disciples expressed worry.

Chat Prompts

- *Be still, and know that I am God! I will be honored by every nation. I will be honored throughout the world.* Psalm 46:10

    When you are overwhelmed with worry, it can be really hard to calm down. You might think that if you keep moving or distracting yourself, you won't have to confront the worry. But this psalm reminds us to slow down and remember who God is. He can do anything! Why does slowing down remind you that God can do anything?

- *For I can do everything through Christ, who gives me strength.* Philippians 4:13

    What does it mean to do things "through Christ"? What do you need strength for today?

- *Can all your worries add a single moment to your life?* Matthew 6:27

    Does worrying about a problem actually solve a problem? Discuss how worry causes problems, but never helps. Make a list of things that do help.

MORE TIME?

Prayer Journal Options

Make a memory about what you read, did, and learned this week.

- Draw ropes and at each end, write something to let go of today.
- Draw little *O*s (See below.) and write something God said while you listened.
- Draw ice cubes and write how prayer and God's love can melt away worry.

Family Prayer: Cheerio Prayers

Preparation: Pass out Cheerio cereal.

The holes remind us to open our ears and hearts when we pray. The name *Cheerio* contains the word *cheer* to remind us that God loves a cheerful heart because it's free of worry.

Pick up one Cheerio at a time and think of something that you worry about. Give the worry to God and eat the Cheerio as a sign you let go and it's all gone.

Wrap-Up

Give worries to God because he is always listening and ready to give you peace.

How Can I Stop My Anger?

Week 18

Family Beatitude: Happy is the family who forgives others, for they will release anger.

Focus: Let go of anger.

Weekly Bible Verse: *Do not let sin control the way you live; do not give in to sinful desires.* Romans 6:12

Activity Options

- ☐ Blow up a balloon until it pops. Discuss what caused it to explode. How can anger inside you cause an outburst?

- ☐ Soft moleskin helps heal blisters that were caused by friction from shoes. Kind words soften a heart blistering from hurts. Pour on lots of kind words in your home to keep hearts soft.

- ☐ Discover what stress busters help you control your emotions: laughter, stress balls, slow deep breaths, tapping fingers on the other palm, looking out into the horizon, running or walking, reading, thinking about a happy memory, praising and thanking God, etc. Write your own list or use the list provided when needed.

Angry Daniel 2 minutes

Daniel had been living at his foster family's house for a couple months. He liked the neighborhood, and had even befriended Charlie from next door. But sometimes Charlie annoyed him.

One day, Daniel walked in the door and screamed, "I want to punch Charlie."

His foster mom Leanne asked, "What would that do?"

"It would make me feel less angry and hurt him back."

"Is that a good thing? Would that help you be friends?"

"No. That's why I didn't do it. But, Leanne, it's hard to stop my anger. I clench my fists. I take slow breaths. I try to recall a joke, and I still feel like a balloon about to burst."

"It's natural to feel hurt and angry, but self-control like you used today is what God wants. Let's pray." They prayed for God's help and Daniel went to read his Bible.

A few minutes later, Daniel ran to Leanne. He said, "God put a verse in my mind. It's Romans 6:12. It tells me not to let sin or evil control me. My new strategy is to think, 'evil you are trashed and not in control.'"

"That's great!" Leanne encouraged, "Try to keep that verse in mind next time you feel angry."

Daniel nodded.

Bible Story Connection 3–4 minutes

Read Acts 9:1-19 about a great church leader who had an anger issue until he encountered Jesus. Talk about his change.

Chat Prompts

- *Don't worry about anything; instead, pray about everything. Tell God what you need, and thank him for all he has done.* Philippians 4:6

    We are bound to worry, but instead of letting that worry control us, what does God say to do? Why is it good to share your emotions with God?

- *Get rid of all bitterness, rage, anger, harsh words, and slander, as well as all types of evil behavior.* Ephesians 4:31

    Discuss ways to get rid of anger, lying, and other negative behavior, including replacing anger with good thoughts and kind words.

- *"Don't sin by letting anger control you." Don't let the sun go down while you are still angry.* Ephesians 4:26

    Why is it important to forgive people by the end of the day? How does it help your heart and sleep?

MORE TIME?

Prayer Journal Options

Make a memory about what you read, did, and learned this week.

- Draw an angry fist and list ways to let anger go.
- Draw a balloon and write things that make you angry inside. Outside the balloon write things that help you to calm down.
- Write a Scripture you will pray. Doodle around it as you think about what it means.

Family Prayer: Overcoming Sin

1. For this week's verse, consider two questions: what does it mean to not let sin rule? And what is evil about the sin?
2. Personalize the prayer. For example, "Lord, don't let sin rule in my body that will die. Help me to avoid its evil desires".
3. Read the full chapter (Romans 6) to understand God's perspective and gain insights. If reading the Scripture causes you to want to ask forgiveness for anger or other negative emotional reaction, do it!

Wrap-Up

Anger is not a bad emotion. In fact, when you see injustice, anger is a good reaction. Even Jesus got angry when the holy Temple was used as a market instead of a place of prayer. But be careful that your anger doesn't make you sin or turn into bitterness or resentment. Replace negative emotions with kindness and love.

How Does God Help Me Solve Problems?

Week 19

Family Beatitude: Happy is the family who prays for solutions, for God will guide them.

Focus: God knows your needs.

Weekly Bible Verse: *If you need wisdom, ask our generous God, and he will give it to you. He will not rebuke you for asking.* James 1:5

Activity Options

- [ ] Use different lenses (magnifying, microscope, telescope, etc.) to look at various objects. Each lens lets you see differently (the details, the big picture, etc.). Chat about looking at problems in different ways and talk about what God sees.

- [ ] Decorate pillowcases with fabric markers. Write one Bible verse or prayer to let go of negative emotions before sleeping and one to remind you that God is always with you.

- [ ] Listen to the song "Through Heaven's Eyes" from *The Prince of Egypt*. What does it mean to look at your life through Heaven's eyes?

FAMILY DEVOTION · READ ALOUD

Lost Pencil 2 minutes

Lupe complained, "Mom, I can't find my homework or a pencil."

Mom entered Lupe's room and said, "Look at this mess. No wonder you can't find things. Do you remember Jesus' story about the woman who lost a coin?"*

Lupe nodded. Mom asked, "What did she do?"

Lupe said, "She swept the floor and found it."

"Yes, she cleaned her home. Can you sweep this floor?"

"No, there's too much stuff."

"What should you do before you sweep?"

"Pick up everything and put it all away." Lupe started picking up books, toys, and clothes off the floor. Her mom left her to work.

An hour later, Mom came to check on Lupe. Lupe beamed and said, "I found my homework, pencil, my favorite toy, and the library book I need to return."

Mom smiled, "You even found the floor! It looks great. What did the woman do after she found her coin?"

Lupe said, "She called her friends and they rejoiced."

Mom nodded, "It looks good enough to invite a friend over to play and celebrate." Lupe hugged her mom, and then called a friend.

* Luke 15:8–10

Bible Story Connection 3–4 minutes

Read Nehemiah 1:3; 2:12, 17–18; 6:15. How did Nehemiah identify the problem and what steps did he take?

Chat Prompts

- *So my God gave me the idea to call together all the nobles and leaders of the city, along with the ordinary citizens, for registration. I had found the genealogical record of those who had first returned to Judah.* Nehemiah 7:5

    God placed an answer in Nehemiah's heart that encouraged him. What encourages you to solve a problem?

- *"LORD, help!" they cried in their trouble, and he rescued them from their distress.* Psalm 107:6

    God hears every single one of your prayers. If you ask him for help, he will send it, although many times it's in a way you wouldn't expect. What are some of the ways God has helped you?

- *Dear brothers and sisters, when troubles of any kind come your way, consider it an opportunity for great joy.* James 1:2

    We don't usually consider it a "great joy" to struggle, but what do struggles teach us? Discuss how problems inspire us to find solutions and develop character.

MORE TIME?

Prayer Journal Options

Make a memory about what you read, did, and learned this week.

- Draw a wall (as a reminder of Nehemiah's wall) and list problem-solving tips.
- Draw a lens or glasses. Write a new way to look at a problem.
- Draw a smile and what you learned from a past problem.

Family Prayer: S-O-A-P Method

If you have a problem, use S-O-A-P to clean it up. Find Bible passage(s) about a similar problem (use a concordance) and do each step below.

Scripture: Read the passage(s) a few times and see what pops out.

Observation: Note what solution helped in the Bible and what things were a hindrance.

Application: Consider how to apply the Bible wisdom to your problem.

Prayer: Pray for God to guide you.

Wrap-Up

God can solve problems in unexpected ways. He spoke to Nehemiah's heart and gave him solutions for the wall. Listen to Bible wisdom.

How Does Forgiveness Help Me?

Week 20

Family Beatitude: Happy is the family who keeps prayer lines open, for they will remain close to God.

Focus: Forgiving others helps you, too!

Weekly Bible Verse: *Don't let evil conquer you, but conquer evil by doing good.* Romans 12:21

Activity Options

- [ ] Take two empty tubes (gift wrap or paper towel). Stuff one with dirty socks. Hold one up to someone's ear and speak into it. Try with the other one. Which one works better?

- [ ] Compare hard and soft materials. Check out how water softens a hard sponge or packed dirt. How does forgiveness soften hearts?

- [ ] Read John 7:37–39. Drink water and ask the Holy Spirit to help you forgive others.

Bully Brise 2 minutes

Will was on his way to the after-school-pick-up line, when he saw Brise. Will ducked his head and hurried to his mom's car.

Brise was known to pull down kid's pants to show their underwear. He pushed people in line. Once he got mad that one kid had a higher test score than he did. He walked up to that boy and kicked him in one shin so hard that he fractured the bone.

Will flung the car door open and jumped inside a little breathless. Mom raised a brow, "Escaping Brise, again?"

Will nodded. "Mom, why do you think Brise is so mean?"

Mom sighed. "Sometimes people are mean to others, because someone else is mean to them. I wonder if he has a hard time at home and feels unloved."

"That would be sad, but could that really make him mean?"

"When your brother fights with you, or doesn't let you play with him when a friend visits, how do you feel?"

"I feel hurt, and then I get mad at him. Sometimes I try to hurt him." Will paused. "Oh. I get it. When I feel hurt and left out, I get a little mean, too."

The next day, Brise tried to bully Will. Will looked at Brise and said, "I'm sorry if you are not happy and if someone is not nice to you. But I know that God loves you no matter what. You might not believe me, but it's true."

Brise turned away and left. Will thought he saw Brise wipe a tear off his face. Brise didn't try to bother Will again, but Will started to pray for Brise.

Bible Story Connection 3–4 minutes

Read John 11:1–44. Discuss doubts people had and how doubts can also block prayer answers.

Chat Prompts

- *Make allowance for each other's faults, and forgive anyone who offends you. Remember, the Lord forgave you, so you must forgive others.* Colossians 3:13

    Making an allowance for other people's faults means that you are merciful when someone does something wrong. Mercy helps you forgive others. Discuss how God forgives those who forgive others.

MORE TIME?

- *If I had not confessed the sin in my heart, the Lord would not have listened.* Psalm 66:18

    When we do something wrong, we need to confess it to God. God wants us to tell him everything, and if we don't, he will know. Chat about how sin blocks our prayers.

- *So he did only a few miracles there because of their unbelief.* Matthew 13:58

    When Jesus went back to his hometown of Nazareth, the people did not believe that he was the Messiah. Because of the people's unbelief, he didn't perform many miracles. Why is faith and not doubting important? How can doubt hinder prayer?

Prayer Journal Options

Make a memory about what you read, did, and learned this week.

- Draw a cross and write about Jesus dying to forgive our sins.
- Draw a maze and list things that block prayers.
- Draw something soft and write about keeping your heart tender.

Family Prayer: 4-Give Reminders

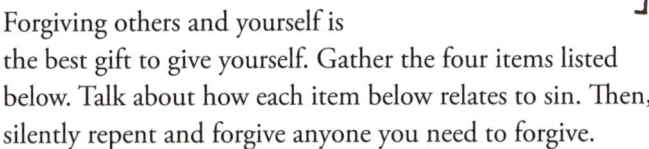

Forgiving others and yourself is the best gift to give yourself. Gather the four items listed below. Talk about how each item below relates to sin. Then, silently repent and forgive anyone you need to forgive.

- **Cotton ball:** Forgiveness softens your heart as it removes anger, pain, and stress.
- **Small yield sign:** Your sins are forgiven when you forgive.
- **Soap or sponge:** Forgiveness cleanses you and keeps the connection to God open.
- **Small weight:** Forgiveness lifts weight off you and gives problem to God.

Wrap-Up

Forgiveness releases you from holding onto pain. When you aren't holding onto anger, bitterness, resentment, or other hurts, you are free to be kind, loving, and patient.

Is a Short Prayer Okay?

Week 21

Family Beatitude: Happy is the family who uses quick prayers for fast needs, for they know everything is possible for God.

Focus: SOS prayers

Weekly Bible Verse: *We will receive from him whatever we ask because we obey him and do the things that please him.* 1 John 3:22

Activity Options

- [ ] Set a timer for one minute. Try to accomplish as many small tasks as possible before the timer goes off. Some ideas might be: washing hands, running fast, or microwaving a snack. Then, spend at least one minute praying.

- [ ] Morse code was created to send quick messages during wartime. Search online for Morse code. Then, send notes to each other. You may already be familiar with SOS (··· − − − ···).

- [ ] Peter prayed one of the shortest prayers in the Bible when he began sinking in the Sea of Galilee. Read Matthew 14:30–31. What did Peter pray? How did Jesus respond?

Parking Spaces 2 minutes

Carmen's older brother, Carlos was a star athlete on the high school soccer team. Today was the final game and Carmen and her mom were in a rush to pick up the cake and get to the field. When Mom's car pulled into the bakery's parking lot, Carmen's heart sank. "Mama, there aren't any parking spots! How will we make it to the game?"

"Let's pray: Lord, help us find the perfect parking spot."

"Look, there's one!" Mom headed to it, but someone else got it. "Mama, why didn't God let us have that one?"

"He knows what's best." A car pulled out by the closest space to the bakery. Mom parked.

"God did have better place for us. Thank you, Father," Mom smiled. They quickly picked up the cake and drove off. The parking lot at the field was also packed. They drove around but found no parking spots.

Carrie said, "Mama, I'll pray for another parking place. Help, God! We need a parking spot. We trust you to have the right one." They drove around again and spotted one, but Mom waved to another driver to take it.

"Mama, why did you let that car take our spot?" Carmen asked.

Mom smiled, "They have a handicapped license plate, but the handicapped places are taken. They need it more." Mom drove around the corner and a car pulled out. She pulled in.

Carmen said, "It's the farthest spot from the field, but I'm glad you helped someone."

Bible Story Connection 3–4 minutes

Read Nehemiah 2:1–10. How did Nehemiah please God with his quick prayer. Note how God answered it quickly. What did the king do?

Chat Prompts

- *"You don't have enough faith," Jesus told them. "I tell you the truth, if you had faith even as small as a mustard seed, you could say to this mountain, 'Move from here to there,' and it would move. Nothing would be impossible."* Matthew 17:20

    A mustard seed is about one to two millimeters in diameter. That's a little bigger than a letter on a penny. You only need a little faith and a short prayer to see God's blessings. Discuss the short prayer Jesus suggested.

- *The king asked, "Well, how can I help you?" With a prayer to the God of heaven, I replied, "If it please the king, and if you are pleased with me, your servant, send me to Judah to rebuild the city where my ancestors are buried."* Nehemiah 2:4–5

    Nehemiah was sad that Jerusalem was in ruins. He had no idea how to restore it. When the king noticed Nehemiah's sadness, he asked how he could help. Before Nehemiah answered, what did he do? Why did he do it?

MORE TIME?

Prayer Journal Options

Make a memory about what you read, did, and learned this week.

- Draw praying hands. Write a short prayer.
- Draw a car. Write how God cares about little needs.
- Draw socks or shoes. Write how God directs your steps.

Family Prayer: S-O-S Prayers

We call 911 for medical emergencies because it is short and easy to remember. We ask Jesus for help when we have a big need, too. Think of S-O-S as "Savior on Site" since Christ is always present. Use simple words and trust God to hear your prayers.

Dear Jesus, help me with _____.

Choose a simple signal to let family members know you need prayer now.

Wrap-Up

Short prayers are absolutely OK! God hears every single prayer no matter how long or short. When you need something say a quick prayer.

What Prayers Are in the Bible?

Week 22

Family Beatitude: Happy is the family who prays like people in the Bible, for their prayers will accomplish much.

Focus: Prayers in the Bible

Weekly Bible Verse: *All Scripture is inspired by God and is useful to teach us what is true and to make us realize what is wrong in our lives. It corrects us when we are wrong and teaches us to do what is right.* 2 Timothy 3:16

Activity Options

- ☐ Draw a picture of the scene Psalm 23 describes. Write the verses from Psalm 23 on the back of the page, using the following colors for specific words: gray for sheep; green for pastures or meadows; blue for water; brown for paths, rod, or staff; black for evil, darkness, or shadows; red for Good Shepherd (willing to die for sheep); yellow for cup or eternity.

- ☐ Take a drive and if it is safe, pull a U-turn or find another unexpected way to get back to your destination. What does it mean to make a U-turn in life?

- ☐ Watch the sunset and pray for tomorrow. How is every day like a fresh start?

Prayer Journal 2 minutes

Savona said, "Daddy, does God really listen to my prayers?"

Daddy said, "Well, let's check out our family prayer journal to find out." Daddy got the book from the shelf and they started turning the pages.

"Daddy, that's when we read about Noah and the flood," Savona pointed. "We wrote that we needed more rain for the plants and animals." Daddy nodded and turned the page to a drawing with rain and flowers.

"I remember God sent rain and the flowers grew and the grass turned green."

Savona nodded and they looked at more pages. She had drawn a picture of Grandma when she fell and hurt her hip. On the page beside it there was a big heart and a flower to thank God for healing Grandma. That page also had drawings of the time Peter healed a lame man.

Savona said, "God answered our prayer when he healed Grandma, just like Peter healed the lame man."

"Yes. God listens to our prayers and answers them." The next page had Jesus written on a big heart.

Savona said, "That's when I told Jesus I love him. I believe he died for me. So I know I'll go to Heaven to be with him one day."

"Savona, does this book remind you that God listens to our prayers?"

Savona beamed, "Yes. I want to look at every page and thank God for all the prayers he heard and all the answers he already sent."

Bible Story Connection 3–4 minutes

David wrote many Psalms that can be sung or prayed. Read Psalm 3:1–7. What did David pray for?

Chat Prompts

- *Your word is a lamp to guide my feet and a light for my path.* Psalm 119:105

    How does a lamp help when you are in the dark? How can God's Word guide us in how to pray?

- *Praise the LORD, the God of Israel, who lives from everlasting to everlasting! And all the people shouted "Amen!" and praised the LORD.* 1 Chronicles 16:36

    The word *amen* is often said at the end of prayers, but do you know what it means? It means *so be it*. It is a way of letting others know that you agree with the prayer. Why did the Israelites shout "Amen"?

- *Jesus often withdrew to the wilderness for prayer.* Luke 5:16

    Even Jesus took time to be alone and pray. Why is it important to build a prayer habit? How can you make prayer a habit?

MORE TIME?

Prayer Journal Options

Make a memory about what you read, did, and learned this week.

- Draw a Bible and name one Bible person who prayed.
- Draw a light and write how God's Word acts as a light.
- Draw a lamb and write how Jesus cares for you and listens.

Wrap-Up

There are many prayer examples in the Bible to follow when building your own prayer habits.

Family Prayer: Bible Prayers

Below are some examples of Bible prayers. Read the passage, discuss it, and pray about it.

Bonus: Read the passage and have children guess who prayed it.

Verses	Who Prayed	Type of Prayer
1 Kings 8:22–24	Solomon	Adoration
1 Samuel 2:1–10	Hannah	Thanksgiving
Nehemiah 1:5–11	Nehemiah	Confession/Help
Jeremiah 17:14	Jeremiah	Healing for Self
Psalm 3:1–7	King David	Deliverance from Enemies
Ephesians 3:14–20	Paul	Intercession
Psalm 139:23–24	King David	Transformation
Numbers 6:22–26	Aaron	Blessing Others
Psalm 25:1–6	King David	Guidance/Protection
1 Samuel 1:10–11	Hannah	Vows (sacred promise)

Can God Help Me with Bullies?

Week 23

Family Beatitude: Happy is the family who trusts that God is stronger than bullies, for they will develop "God" esteem.

Focus: Bully busters

Weekly Bible Verse: *The Lord is faithful; he will strengthen you and guard you from the evil one.* 2 Thessalonians 3:3

Activity Options

- ☐ Weight lift with water bottles and do other muscle strengthening exercises. Discuss how prayer practice increases spiritual muscle power.

- ☐ Write your feelings about a bully. Stomp on the paper and say, "The devil and bullies have no power over me." Crumple the paper, trash it, and say, "Jesus and the truth set me free."

- ☐ When a bully says mean things to you, replace their words with Scripture or thoughts of God and people who love you.

Soccer Bully Busting 2 minutes

Michael fell down on the soccer field. A player on the opposing team had kicked him hard in the ankle. His dad carried him off the field. At the ER, the doctor sad, "It's a bad sprain, but nothing's broken. Stay off that foot for a week."

Later, Michael told Dad, "I heard the other coach tell that player to get me out. They hurt me on purpose."

"Let's pray that doesn't happen again," Dad suggested.

Michael prayed with Dad. They asked God for wisdom against the bullies. The next time Michael played that team, he was prepared. He watched that team play and saw how players attacked opponents. One player ran toward him. Once he got close, Michael turned sideways as the player lifted his foot to kick. The player missed Michael and flipped onto his back. Later, two players ran toward him and he stepped back just before they came close. The players rammed into one another and fell down.

The coach of the opposing team yelled to the referees that Michael had tried to hurt his players. The line referee said, "He did nothing. In fact, he stepped out of the way to protect himself. It appeared that your players were aiming to hurt him. You better tell your players to play fair. I'll be watching."

Bible Story Connection 3–4 minutes

Read Luke 10:25–37, a story about a man who helped someone who was beaten by bullies. How could you help bully victims?

Chat Prompts

- *I tell you, you can pray for anything, and if you believe that you've received it, it will be yours.* Mark 11:24

    Trusting in God will give you strength to resist bullies. How does God's strength do this?

- *Because you are my helper, I sing for joy in the shadow of your wings.* Psalm 63:7

    The writer calls God their helper. Why do you think they are happy to be under God's shadow? What does it mean to be under God's wings?

- *O Lord, rescue me from evil people. Protect me from those who are violent.* Psalm 140:1

    Bible scholars guess that King David wrote this prayer when he was fleeing from his son who wanted his throne. Share Bible stories of God's protection and rescues.

MORE TIME?

Prayer Journal Options

Make a memory about what you read, did, and learned this week.

- Draw a feather or wings. Write about God's protection.
- Draw weights. Write about growing prayer muscles.
- Trace your hand. Write about the Handy Bully Buster Prayer (below).

Family Prayer: Handy Bully Buster Prayer

Let your hand guide your prayer for protection.

- Thumbs up—Ask Almighty God for protection.
- Pointer finger—Thank God for your good points (your talents and character) and point out the problem to God.
- Middle finger— Pray for wisdom to find middle ground of a safer place to go.
- Ring finger—Ask God for a ring of friends to help protect one another.
- Little finger—A little forgiveness goes a long way, so forgive bullies.

Hold up your hand and ask God to "Stop the Bullying." Pray for courage to wave goodbye, turn, and leave when bullies show up.

Wrap-Up

Pray for God's protection when you encounter a bully. Be like a Good Samaritan when you see a victim of bullying.

Can I Trust God?

Week 24

Family Beatitude: Happy is the family who knows faith grows as they exercise it, for they will move mountains.

Focus: Building faith

Weekly Bible Verse: *Trust in the Lord with all your heart; do not depend on your own understanding.* Proverbs 3:5

Activity Options

- ☐ Look at a coin. Coins contain words about trust and God. When you find a coin it's like God whispering, "Trust me." Discuss how coins add up and trust builds.

- ☐ Find a yeast bread recipe. Gather the ingredients. Examine the grains of yeast. Discuss how something tiny has the power to grow and make bread rise. Then, make bread together.

- ☐ Read Matthew 6:19–20. Find things that have rusted, gotten moldy, or developed holes in them. Can you trust broken things?

The Water Slide 2 minutes

"Mom, I want to try the water slide!" said Ben when they arrived at the pool.

Mom eyed the water slide. "First you need to learn to swim." They changed, put their bags down on the benches, and waded into the shallow end. Mom held Ben on top of the water. She said, "I will let go so you can float."

Ben yelled, "No! I'll sink."

"Don't worry, if you lean back, the water will hold you."

Ben gripped the edge of the pool as he watched Mom demonstrate. He still wasn't sure. So he floated a toy boat. They tried again and again. Finally, he floated.

"Great job, Ben!" Mom praised, "You must be so proud of yourself."

"Yea, this isn't so bad!" Ben said cautiously.

Over the next few days, Mom taught Ben to blow bubbles, bob up and down, and kick his feet. Ben learned the doggy paddle and then the breaststroke, too.

One day Ben said, "I'm read for the slide." He climbed the stairs. He looked down, and thought, *This looks scary*. Then another thought rose to his mind; *I can do scary things by trusting in God*.

Ben sat down and pushed forward. *Wosh!* He slid around the curves and plopped into the water. He kicked his legs and pushed his head out of the water, took a deep breath, and swam.

Later Ben said, "Wow, trusting God is like trusting you can float and swim. I just believed God is strong enough." Mom smiled.

Bible Story Connection 3–4 minutes

Read Acts 2. How did the Holy Spirit give Peter courage? How did it help to grow the number of believers?

Chat Prompts

- *Now all glory to God, who is able, through his mighty power at work within us, to accomplish infinitely more than we might ask or think.* Ephesians 3:20

    Have you ever thought about how strange it is that God wants to "work within us"? He is all-powerful, but he asks us to trust him so that he can accomplish more than we can ever imagine. Discuss God's ability to answer prayers.

- *Dear friends,* [you] *must build each other up in your most holy faith, pray in the power of the Holy Spirit.* Jude 1:20

    What does it mean to build up each other's faith? Discuss ways you are building your faith.

- *I pray that God, the source of hope, will fill you completely with joy and peace because you trust in him. Then you will overflow with confident hope through the power of the Holy Spirit.* Romans 15:13

    God wants to fill you up with joy and peace. How do you feel when you are overflowing with the Holy Spirit?

MORE TIME?

Prayer Journal Options

Make a memory about what you read, did, and learned this week.

- Draw a building and list how you build your faith.
- Draw water and write about swimming and trust.
- Draw coins. Write about increasing faith.

Wrap-Up

You can trust God by believing in his promises in the Bible. Trusting God will lead to big blessings!

Family Prayer: R-I-C-H-E-R

Build a R-I-C-H-E-R prayer life with this acrostic method.

What	How	Pray
Read	Read a passage and note what impresses you.	Thank God for the message.
Insights	Consider the meaning.	Pray for God's wisdom.
Challenge	Challenge yourself to apply the truth.	Pray about applying the words.
Hope	Reflect on how the passage brings hope.	Thank God for the hope you find.
Evaluate	Evaluate your choices in light of God's Word.	Ask God to show you any changes to make.
Relationships	Consider how the message helps you relate to people and God.	Ask God to share the hope found.

What's a Prayer Buddy?

Week 25

Family Beatitude: Happy is the family that prays together, for they will be accountable.

Focus: Prayer partners

Weekly Bible Verse: *Let us think of ways to motivate one another to acts of love and good works.* Hebrews 10:24

Activity Options

- ☐ Try lifting something very heavy by yourself, and then try lifting it with someone else. Was it easier? Try using a seesaw or playing catch alone, and then with someone else. Was it easier? How does teamwork make things better?

- ☐ Pair up for tasks like cleaning a bathroom, weeding, or washing a car. How is sharing the load faster and more fun?

- ☐ Try to do pull ups on the monkey b alone. Then, have an adult or older sibling lift you from the waist. Did teamwork make it easier?

Prayer Buddies 2 minutes

Maddy was quiet the whole way home from church. She ignored her sister Lacey when she tried to get her to sing along to the radio. By the time they got home and went up to their room, Lacey had had enough of the silent treatment.

"OK, Maddy, spill it. What's wrong?" Lacey asked.

Maddy sighed, "We learned about prayer buddies in church today. And Kaden and I decided to be buddies."

"That's great!" Lacey exclaimed, "You are such great friends."

Maddy nodded, but didn't smile. "Yeah, we are good friends, but later on, his team won the Bible trivia game and he rubbed it in my face. Now, I don't think we can be prayer buddies."

Lacey gave her sister a hug. When she pulled back she said, "We fight sometimes, right?" Maddy nodded. Lacey continued, "But we are still sisters and we still care about each other, right?" Maddy nodded. "So, I think you can still be prayer buddies with Kaden, but you'll need to forgive one another. You will also need to be happy when your buddy wins a game because buddies are happy when their buddy is blessed."

Maddy smiled and said, "That's hard, but I'll pray that I can be happy for Kaden. Thanks, Sis."

Bible Story Connection 3–4 minutes

Read Nehemiah 4:15–20. How did teamwork help the work continue despite threats from enemies? How is teamwork like prayer buddies?

Chat Prompts

- *[Jesus] called his twelve disciples together and began sending them out two by two, giving them authority to cast out evil spirits.* Mark 6:7

  Why do you think the disciples were sent out in groups of two? Discuss how parents pray together and how children can pray with each other or with a close friend.

MORE TIME?

- *When we get together, I want to encourage you in your faith, but I also want to be encouraged by yours.* Romans 1:12

  Name some people who encourage your faith. What about their faith is encouraging? How could a pray buddy encourage you?

- *Dear brothers and sisters, I urge you in the name of our Lord Jesus Christ to join in my struggle by praying to God for me. Do this because of your love for me, given to you by the Holy Spirit.* Romans 15:30

  What do you learn about praying for a prayer buddy from this verse?

Prayer Journal Options

Make a memory about what you read, did, and learned this week.

- Draw hearts and write about praying together.
- Draw a mouth and write encouraging words.
- Trace your buddy's hand and write ways to pray for that person.

Family Prayer: Prayer Buddies

Pray regularly with a family member or friend to encourage each other.

- Each buddy lists their prayer concerns and blessings.
- Pray for your buddy's prayer needs.
- Praise God for answers and blessings.
- Agree to be encouraging, speak truth lovingly, and share ideas to grow in faith.
- Be responsible: pray for your buddy every day.

Wrap-Up

A prayer buddy is someone who prays for you and who encourages you to pray. Pray with a prayer buddy to keep your spiritual life strong.

How Is Singing like Praying?

Week 26

Family Beatitude: Happy is the family who sings praises, for they will have a melody in their hearts.

Focus: Singing as prayer

Weekly Bible Verse: *Then I will praise God's name with singing, and I will honor him with thanksgiving.* Psalm 69:30

Activity Options

- ☐ Listen to a song. Share what words bring joy or help you pray.
- ☐ Choose a favorite Scripture and add a tune to create a song.
- ☐ Dance or do hand motions to praise music as another form of worship.

Dance Praise Party
2 minutes

Momma called the children and said, "You all did a great job cleaning. Let's have a party."

Rebecca asked, "Is it someone's birthday?"

"No." Papa said, "This is the day the Lord has made."

The children shouted the rest of the verse: "Let us rejoice and be glad in it."

Mattias asked, "Is there a cake?"

"We have some treats. First let's turn on music and march around." The children grabbed instruments and played to the music. Papa sang and led them around.

Momma said, "Singing praise is praying with music." They sat and clapped to the next song, and then took turns calling out a reason to praise God.

Daisy started with saying, "God made today."

After a few more songs Momma said, "Time for a snack break. We have popcorn, fruit slices, candy, and lemonade."

Everyone shouted, "Hooray!"
Papa prayed over the food.

Mattias said, "God makes every day. Can we have a praise party every day?"

Daddy said, "A praise party is just one way to praise God. Tomorrow, let's see what else we can do to praise God."

Bible Story Connection 3–4 minutes

Read Exodus 15:1–21 when Miriam and the Israelites sang and danced to thank God. What did they sing about?

Chat Prompts

- *Be filled with the Holy Spirit, singing psalms and hymns and spiritual songs among yourselves, and making music to the Lord in your hearts.* Ephesians 5:18–19

    According to this verse, what does being filled with the Holy Spirit mean? What do you like about singing to God and one another?

MORE TIME?

- *Are any of you suffering hardships? You should pray. Are any of you happy? You should sing praises.* James 5:13

    This verse gives some good advice for when you are happy or when you are sad. How do your feelings make a difference in prayer?

- *Sing a new song of praise to him; play skillfully on the harp, and sing with joy.* Psalm 33:3

    In Bible times, harps were used for praise and worship. What instruments does your worship team use? You can make your own instruments with pots and pans. Try to turn this verse into a joyful song.

Prayer Journal Options

Make a memory about what you read, did, and learned this week.

- Draw a musical note symbol and write about singing to God.
- Write words you'd like to make into a song.
- Draw a musical instrument and write why you like the sounds it makes.

Family Prayer: Sing-spiration

Get inspired with music! Singspirations began in the 1980s at Biola University's chapel. People gather together to sing psalms, hymns, and spiritual songs. Plan your own singspiration night and make a playlist of your favorite Christian songs. Turn it on and sing along! Pause at times to shout reasons to praise God or to pray for a need.

Wrap-Up

Praying is communicating with God and singing is a way to worship God. Use songs to pray!

What If I Don't Know What to Pray?

Week 27

Family Beatitude: Happy is the family who doesn't know what to pray, for the Holy Spirit will pray for them.

Focus: The Holy Spirit prays for us

Weekly Bible Verse: *The Holy Spirit helps us in our weakness. For example, we don't know what God wants us to pray for. But the Holy Spirit prays for us with groanings that cannot be expressed in words.* Romans 8:26

Activity Options

- [ ] Set up an obstacle course. Blindfold a volunteer and have another person guide the volunteer through the obstacle course. How is walking blindly through an obstacle course like trusting the Holy Spirit?

- [ ] Make a fruit salad and eat it together. Share how the Holy Spirit also gives us the fruit of the Spirit (Galatians 5:22–23).

- [ ] Play with magnets and magnetic objects. How is the Holy Spirit like a magnet who sticks with us?

Blindfolded 2 minutes

For family night, Aamira and Nael's parents set up an obstacle course in the backyard. They blindfolded Aamira and told Nael to guide her. Aamira said, "I'm afraid I will fall or bump into something."

"Don't worry," Nael reassured her. "I'm your guide like the Holy Spirit. I'll help you. Step to the right to miss the rock. Put your hand out and feel the ladder. Climb up three steps and back down." Aamira followed the directions.

Nael said, "Feel that paper? There's a prayer to read."

"I can't see the words," Aamira objected.

"I'll read and say them for you," Nael offered. After the prayer, Nael led Aamira around obstacles, under a bench, over a puddle, and around some trees. He held her hand when she needed walk in a straight line, too.

Aamira made it to the end and took off her blindfold. She looked back and said, "Wow! I made it through it all. Now it's your turn Nael."

Aamira covered Nael's eyes. Then she helped her parents move things around into a new obstacle course. Before they started again Nael said, "This feels weird. I can't see anything. I thought it would be easy, but I have to trust you Aamira."

"Yep, just trust me like you trust the Holy Spirit."

Their parents smiled and watched their children complete the trust course.

Bible Story Connection 3–4 minutes

Read Acts 8:26–40. How did the Holy Spirit guide Philip?

Chat Prompts

- *When the Father sends the Advocate as my representative—that is, the Holy Spirit—he will teach you everything and will remind you of everything I have told you.* John 14:26

    Jesus promised his disciples that they would not be alone when they preached the Good News. Who would be with them? Look up the word advocate in the dictionary and read the definition. How is the Holy Spirit like an advocate?

- *None of them could stand against the wisdom and the Spirit with which Stephen spoke.* Acts 6:10

    Stephen was the first person in the Bible to die for his faith in Jesus. He spoke with wisdom that others could not argue against. The Holy Spirit guided many early Christians and still does, today. Pray for the Holy Spirit to give you wisdom like Stephen.

- *With Christ as my witness, I speak with utter truthfulness. My conscience and the Holy Spirit confirm it.* Romans 9:1

    Chat about praying for the Holy Spirit to reveal truth when you are confused.

MORE TIME?

Prayer Journal Options

Make a memory about what you read, did, and learned this week.

- Draw a dove, which is a symbol of the Holy Spirit, and list facts about the Holy Spirit.

- Draw a blindfold. List ways the Holy Spirit guides us.

- Draw fruit and lists the Fruit of the Spirit.

Family Prayer: Prayer Hand Stack

Stack your hands. To start, one person puts their hand on the table. Another person puts their hand on top of the first person's hand. Continue until each person has a hand in the stack.

The person with a hand on the bottom pulls it out and places it on the top of the stack as they either say a few words of prayer or simply say "Holy Spirit pray for me." Continue as long as desired.

Wrap-Up

If you don't know what to pray, ask the Holy Spirit to guide you.

What Is the Fear of the Lord?

Week 28

Family Beatitude: Happy is the family who fears God, for they understand his power.

Focus: Fear of God

Weekly Bible Verse: *God is powerful and dreadful. He enforces peace in the heavens.* Job 25:2

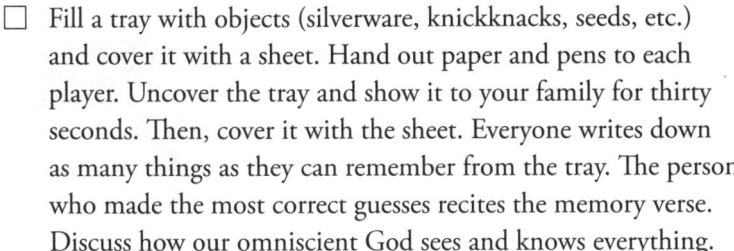

Activity Options

- ☐ Look at a knife. How can it be used for good? How can it be dangerous?

- ☐ Fill a tray with objects (silverware, knickknacks, seeds, etc.) and cover it with a sheet. Hand out paper and pens to each player. Uncover the tray and show it to your family for thirty seconds. Then, cover it with the sheet. Everyone writes down as many things as they can remember from the tray. The person who made the most correct guesses recites the memory verse. Discuss how our omniscient God sees and knows everything.

- ☐ Use the hearts from the page 128 to make a mobile. You'll have a hanging prayer tool.

Fearsome God 2 minutes

Christopher watched Dad fold his uniform. "Dad, you're a soldier. I bet you're not afraid of anything."

Dad smirked. "That's not true. I fear God."

"But God loves you. There's no reason to be afraid."

Dad pulled a switchblade from his pocket. "Look at this knife. It cuts fruit, but it can also cut me. It is a useful but dangerous tool. I don't throw it or grab it by the blade. It reminds me of God."

Christopher scrunched up his face. "How is God like a knife?"

"God's Word is sharper than a knife or sword with double edges. It cuts through my bad thoughts. It reminds me to obey God and keep me from sinning."

Christopher shifted his weight. "God won't hurt me, right?"

"No," Dad smiled, "God loves you, but God is holy. Sin separates us from God. God will judge sinners after they die."

"That's why I ask God to forgive me."

"Yes. God always will forgive you if you ask. Reading the Bible helps us know what displeases God."

"Let's read it now," Christopher suggested.

Bible Story Connection 3–4 minutes

Read Exodus 1:15–22 and compare fear of God with other fears.

Chat Prompts

MORE TIME?

- *You have tested my thoughts and examined my heart in the night. You have scrutinized me and found nothing wrong. I am determined not to sin in what I say.* Psalm 17:3

    David asked God to test him and to examine his thoughts and heart. God found nothing wrong with him and David was determined not to sin with his words. Why can God testing your heart give you joy and fear?

- *I'll tell you whom to fear. Fear God, who has the power to kill you and then throw you into hell. Yes, he's the one to fear.* Luke 12:5

    To fear God means to honor and respect him. How can you respect God? How can you disrespect God? What are God's greatest powers?

- *Those who know your name trust in you, for you, O LORD, do not abandon those who search for you.* Psalm 9:10

    You trust in those whom you respect. What happens when you trust in God?

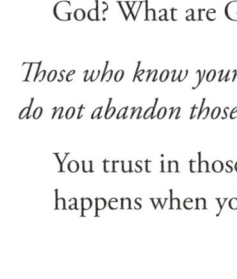

Prayer Journal Options

Make a memory about what you read, did, and learned this week.

- Draw an eye and write things God sees you do.
- Draw a knife and describe fear of the Lord.
- Draw a heart and write about God's love.

> **Wrap-Up**
> Fear God by honoring and respecting him.

Family Prayer: Heart Design Prayers

Make paper hearts picturing truths about God. Use them to adore God and understand the Fear of the Lord.

What to Draw on Heart	What It Symbolizes	What to Pray
Knife or battery	These are helpful but powerful items.	Thank God for loving you. Thank him for being so powerful and punishing the wicked.
Crown	God is King.	Pray for help to obey the King's rules.
Eyes	God sees all we do and think.	Thank God for watching over you and ask forgiveness for sins.
Heart	Be open to God's love and know he has a hedge of protection around us.	Love God and thank him for protecting you.
Sword (Hebrews 4:12)	God's Word is powerful.	Thank God for his Word that's sharper than swords to cut through our negative thoughts.

What Can God Do?

Week 29

Family Beatitude: Happy is the family who trusts God's abilities, for they will have great faith.

Focus: Trust God is almighty

Weekly Bible Verse: *Jesus looked at them intently and said, "Humanly speaking, it is impossible. But with God everything is possible."* Matthew 19:26

Activity Options

☐ Plant several types of seeds. Observe how they grow at different rates.

☐ Examine mustard seeds and consider Matthew 17:20.

☐ Read the Apostle's Creed and consider how the words are like seeds of faith.

Planting Seeds 2 minutes

Luna planted basil seeds in an egg carton. She watered the seeds every day. One day, they sprouted.

Her stepmom Liz said, "Did you know that planting is like faith?"

Luna squinted at her, "What do you mean?"

"When you trust God, you plant a seed of faith in your heart. You water the faith by reading God's Word," Liz explained. Luna thought about this over the next few days.

When the basil grew, they moved some plants into flower pots. Then they moved the ones too big for the pots to the garden.

"Will the faith in my heart get too big, too?" Luna asked.

Liz chuckled. "Your faith will overflow, and people will notice it. God answers prayers when we have faith."

Luna said, "We have more basil plants than we need. I will give some to our neighbors."

She put the potted plants in her wagon and she and Liz wheeled it to nearby houses. Luna told Mrs. Molokwu, "This is basil for cooking. You can add it to sauces, salads, and even put it on baked bread. I planted the seeds. I also planted faith in my heart. I know God loves you."

Mrs. Molokwu smiled and thanked her.

Bible Story Connection 3–4 minutes

Read and discuss Matthew 13:31–32 and 17:20.
How do faith and logic work together?

Chat Prompts

- *God is so wise and so mighty. Who has ever challenged him successfully?* Job 9:4

    Talk about human power and strength and God's power and strength. We must remember that God cannot sin. He created our world and chose to stay consistent with being himself. He always good, just, and loving in using his power.

MORE TIME?

- *I am the LORD, the God of all peoples of the world. Is anything too hard for me?* Jeremiah 32:27

    God does not break natural laws and science he created. He does not sin or lie (Hebrews 6:18). Discuss how God can do anything that is in his will. Our problems are never too hard for God.

- *A final word: Be strong in the Lord and in his mighty power.* Ephesians 6:10

    How can God give us courage and strength?

Prayer Journal Options

Make a memory about what you read, did, and learned this week.

- Draw seeds and write prayers that will take time.
- Draw weeds and list weeds that grow in hearts.
- Draw the world and write "God can do anything!"

Wrap-Up

Nothing is impossible when you believe in God.

Family Prayer: Garden Prayers

Praying for goals and dreams is like planting seeds because the results take time. Some plants grow slowly. Pray as you sow and care for seeds and the plants.

What to Do	What God Does	What to Pray	What Happens
Plant seeds	Made seeds	For fertile soil of hearts, sprouting growth	God's Word is a seed of truth.
Water	Sends rain	Matthew 19:26 every day	God cleanses our hearts.
Weed	Allows weeds to grow	To pull out weeds of discouragement or impatience	God forgives and removes sin.
Eliminate Pests	Sends pest fighters like lady bugs	For God to remove Satan's influence	Prayer helps us resist temptation.
Harvest	Causes growth	Thank God for results	God helps us grow.

What Is a Prayer Walk?

Week 30

Family Beatitude: Happy is the family who prayer walks, for God walks with them.

Focus: Prayer walks

Weekly Bible Verse: *Mark out a straight path for your feet; stay on the safe path.* Proverbs 4:26

Activity Options

- ☐ On index cards, write the following verses about walking: Genesis 13:17; 48:15, Exodus 14:22, Leviticus 26:12, Deuteronomy 11:22, Psalm 23:4; 40:2; 119:45. Take one with each walk to discuss.

- ☐ Take an A-B-C Creation walk. As you walk through your neighborhood, in alphabetical order, take turns listing something that God created.

- ☐ Play Prayer Hot Potato. Stand or sit in a circle and pass around a soft ball or stuffed animal. When a player takes the toy, they say a quick prayer for someone they know.

- ☐ Wash one another's feet after a walk or enjoy a foot spa time— wash feet, rub with lotion or oil, and apply polish to toenails.

FAMILY DEVOTION · READ ALOUD

Alphabet Walk 2 minutes

Sonya and her brother Kostas held hands as they walked with their grandparents down the street. Sonya called out, "I see an acorn for *A*. I thank God for the oak trees."

Kostas pointed to the sky and yelled, "There's a bird for *B*. Thanks God for caring for the birds and us."

They enjoyed their A-B-C praise walk. Some letters were hard, like *Q*.

"There's a rock with quartz!" Dad pointed out. "Let's praise God for being our rock." They nodded and prayed.

They also found trash as they walked. Sonya put on gloves, picked it up, and put it in a trash bag that Mom carried.

Sonya said, "Let's pray for people to care for the earth God made." They stopped and prayed.

When they got to the park, they played on the swings and seesaw. Mom took out a snack and they sat to enjoy it. Dad read a Scripture about Abraham walking across the land and they talked about it. Mom snapped some photos to add to their scrapbook.

Everyone helped clean up their picnic area and continued the prayer walk. Back home Sonya said, "I want to draw pictures of what we saw." She took out her journal and colored a beautiful picture.

Bible Story Connection 3–4 minutes

Read Luke 24:13–35. What was special about this walk? How would you feel if you were one of the disciples?

Chat Prompts

- *God, the LORD, created the heavens and stretched them out. He created the earth and everything in it. He gives breath to everyone, life to everyone who walks the earth.* Isaiah 42:5

  We can praise God for his creation every single day. What are some things you can praise God for right now?

MORE TIME?

- *How will anyone go and tell them without being sent? That is why the Scriptures say, "How beautiful are the feet of messengers who bring good news!"* Romans 10:15

  Missionaries give up their lives to spread the gospel. How will anyone know about Jesus if his followers don't share the news? Chat about places our feet go and the opportunities to share your faith.

- *Since we are living by the Spirit, let us follow the Spirit's leading in every part of our lives.* Galatians 5:25

  What does it mean to follow the Spirit's leading? Compare walking with staying in step with God and choosing which way to walk.

Prayer Journal Options

Make a memory about what you read, did, and learned this week.

- Trace your foot and write about prayer walks.
- Draw a compass and write about making good choices.
- Draw your head with a thought bubble above it. Write or draw what you saw on your walk.

Family Prayer: Prayer Walks

Prepare to walk as you pray.

- Dress for the weather. Pray at your door for God to bless the walk.
- Let members take turns saying a prayer as you walk around the neighborhood or hike the wilderness.
- Thank God for creation as you walk.
- Pause at beautiful sights to thank God.
- Pray at eyesore spots to consider helping to care for the spot.

Wrap-Up

A prayer walk is when you go for a walk and thank God for what you see. If you see bad things, like litter or broken items, throw them away. Pray wherever you go!

What Does God Want Me to Do Today?

Week 31

Family Beatitude: Happy is the family who prays for daily guidance, for they will live with purpose.

Focus: Purpose

Weekly Bible Verse: *Tune your ears to wisdom, and concentrate on understanding.* Proverbs 2:2

Activity Options

- [ ] Make paper traffic lights. Cut red, green, and yellow circles out of colored construction paper. Glue the circles onto a black construction-paper rectangle with the red circle on top, the yellow in the middle, and the green on the bottom. Punch a hole in the top and string yarn through it to make a door hanger.

- [ ] Do a safety check of your home. Restock the first aid kit. Check your fire extinguisher and smoke detectors. Discuss how to make an internal safety check when confronted with a difficult choice.

- [ ] Discuss daily priorities. List things you need to do as a family and work on it.

Safety First 2 minutes

Caleb said to Uncle Joe, "I did my chores and it's Saturday. Can you help me ride a bicycle?"

"Sure. Let's take a walk."

"But I want to ride, not walk."

Uncle Joe laughed and said, "I know, but we need to pause and think about safety first."

At the end of the driveway Uncle Joe asked, "What would you do on your bike here?"

"I would need to stop and look for people on the sidewalk. Then I can turn and ride on the sidewalk."

"Good choices," Uncle Joe high-fived Caleb.

They continued around the block and talked about different rules and choices. Back home Uncle Joe and Caleb checked out his bicycle. They squeezed tires to see if they had enough air and looked at the chain to be sure it worked well. They made sure the seat was the right height to ride. They took off the training wheels. Uncle Joe prayed for safety and for Caleb to master riding his bicycle.

Caleb got on and started to peddle. He wiggled and the bicycle tipped, but Uncle Joe held the bicycle up. Caleb kept working at balancing and peddling. He tried to brake at the end of the block and almost fell over.

Uncle Joe said, "Think about how long it took you to stop and also when you first noticed the end of the block."

"I get it. I need to look ahead and choose when to slow down."

"Yes. You're getting the hang of it!"

Bible Story Connection 3–4 minutes

Read Ruth 2:1–13; 4:13. Ruth made a hard choice leaving her family behind and following Naomi to her homeland. What else did Ruth do for Naomi?

God blessed Ruth's choice to provide for Naomi and it gave her the opportunity to meet the man she married.

Chat Prompts

- *Give us today the food we need.* Matthew 6:11

    Jesus is the Bread of Life, meaning he supples all your needs. How are needs different than desires?

MORE TIME?

- *Therefore, whenever we have the opportunity, we should do good to everyone—especially to those in the family of faith.* Galatians 6:10

    How could you take time each day to do a good deed to help someone?

- *Live wisely among those who are not believers, and make the most of every opportunity.* Colossians 4:5

    Nonbelievers have a different way of living. It can be tempting to live like them, but remember that ultimate joy and blessing come from God. How can you make the most of each day? Start by thinking about your morning, then your afternoon, and finally, your evening.

Prayer Journal Options

Make a memory about what you read, did, and learned this week.

- Draw bread and write about daily needs and prayers.
- Draw a traffic light and write about a safety rule.

Family Prayer: Traffic Signal Prayers

Traffic signals use red, yellow, and green lights to show us how to be safe. Let those colors be prayer and decision-making signals. Pray the colors when you have choices to make.

- **Red:** Stop and pray for wisdom. Remember Jesus died to set you free, so make choices that keep you free from sin.
- **Yellow:** Be careful and ask God to show you how to avoid temptation and help you stay safe.
- **Green:** Go and do good when you see an opportunity. Pray God will bless your choice and work.

Wrap-Up

Pray for daily guidance so that your choices reflect God's will.

How Do I Thank God?

Week 32

Family Beatitude: Happy is the family that thanks God, for they will be content.

Focus: Gratitude

Weekly Bible Verse: *Be thankful in all circumstances, for this is God's will for you who belong to Christ Jesus.* 1 Thessalonians 5:18

Activity Options

- ☐ Make paper chains of praise. Cut colored construction paper into strips. Write reasons to thank God on the strip. Then, loop them together like a chain.

- ☐ Make cookies or pretzels in the shape of the cross. The cross shape also looks like a *T*, so it will remind you to thank God as you share them with friends and family.

- ☐ Hold a party to thank family members for hard work and prayers. Celebrate with building ice cream sundaes (like in the Family Devotion on p. 142) or pita bread and dips (similar to the Last Supper).

Ice Cream Sundaes 2 minutes

Mom called the family to the kitchen. They saw bowls, cartons of favorite ice cream flavors, sprinkles, nuts, toppings, fruit, and whipped cream.

Mom said, "I want to thank you for all the hard work today with cleaning the house and getting your rooms organized. You got rid of piles of trash. Now you can pile ice cream and toppings high."

Jesse said, "And then I'll get rid of that pile by eating it!" His brothers laughed. They grabbed bowls and started scooping ice cream.

Jesse called out, "Let's see who will build the highest ice cream pile." He added two more scoops to his bowl. Brendon and Dylan kept adding ice cream and toppings until the ice cream started sliding off. Finally, they squirted on whipped cream and started eating.

Mom said, "Some of these piles may be too high to finish at once, but we can freeze what's left. I don't want you to get stomach aches." No one finished their dessert bowl, not even Jesse. They covered them with plastic wrap and put them in the freezer.

Mom said, "Let's thank God for ice cream, for strong arms and legs that can work hard, and for all that God gives us."

Jesse prayed, "Thank you, Father, for my Mom. She's the best and she usually gives me veggies and sometimes sweet treats."

The others added thanks for their home, friends, good health, minds that grew, books, the outdoors, and more.

Bible Story Connection 3–4 minutes

Read Luke 22:7–19 and John 6:10–11.
How did Jesus thank God in these stories?

Chat Prompts

- *Let them praise the LORD for his great love and for the wonderful things he has done for them.* Psalm 107:15

    List wonderful things God has done, and then thank God for everything named.

- *Give thanks to him who alone does mighty miracles.* **His faithful love endures forever.** Psalm 136:4

    Thank God for being a miracle worker. Thank God for the miracles he will do in the future.

- *We always thank God for all of you and pray for you constantly.* 1 Thessalonians 1:2

    Thank God for the people in your life and pray for God to bless them.

MORE TIME?

Prayer Journal Options

Make a memory about what you read, did, and learned this week.

- Draw ice-cream cones and write a thank-you note to Jesus.
- Draw or write names of people in your life for whom you are thankful.
- Make a prayer chain like the one on page 141 and list reasons to thank God.

Family Prayer: Praying Over Greeting Cards

Take out Christmas, birthday, and other cards family members have received and saved. Take each card one at a time and pray for the person(s) who sent them. Thank God for each person and send each one a card to let them know your family is praying for them.

Wrap-Up

It is important to thank God every day. If you stop praying and thanking God, you begin to take credit for your own success and you may become ungrateful when things don't work out the way you want. Giving thanks helps you keep a positive perspective because you know that God is in control.

Does God Help When I Hurt?

Week 33

Family Beatitude: Happy is the family who gives their hurts to God, for they will learn to comfort others.

Focus: Empathy

Weekly Bible Verse: *"Don't let your hearts be troubled. Trust in God, and trust also in me."* John 14:1

Activity Options

- [ ] Have a Teddy bear or stuffed animal party. Set up chairs for the toys with plates and cups. Celebrate the snuggly little bundles of softness that comfort you.

- [ ] Convert empty pill bottles into comfort bottles. Fill them with rolled-up verses about comfort (Psalm 23:4, Psalm 71:21, Psalm 94:19, Matthew 5:4, 2 Corinthians 1:4, etc.). Search online for more Bible verses about God's comfort.

- [ ] Collect and share *God incidents*—stories about God's comfort and healing.

Tongue Tied 2 minutes

Riley ran to her teacher for ask for help, but blood gushed out instead of words. She'd been playing on the monkey bars, lost her grip and fell—hard. Her tongue was between her teeth when she'd fallen chin-first into the playground sand. The teacher scooped her up and raced to the nurse.

The next thing Riley recalled was sitting in the dentist chair as her parents rushed in. They held her hands. Her tongue was too swollen to speak.

"She bit through her tongue," the nurse explained. "She's going to need oral surgery, and we don't have anyone qualified. We'll need to transfer you to a different facility."

A few hours later, at the new facility, a group of men in lab coats walked in Riley's room. One smiled and said, "Hello. They call me Mad Dog Jack. I'm going to stitch your tongue."

Riley opened her eyes wide as her dad squeezed her hand, and said, "It will be OK."

Mad Dog Jack explained, "I'm an oral surgeon. We have a dental convention here this week, so other oral surgeons are with me. They want to watch how I stitch your tongue in case they need to do it sometime. You just made our conference more exciting. It's lucky we were here."

Mom whispered to Riley, "It's not luck. We prayed this morning for God to provide what we needed today, and he did."

Bible Story Connection 3–4 minutes

Read 2 Kings 4:1–7. How did God use Elisha to keep a widow and her sons from starving?

Chat Prompts

- *No discipline is enjoyable while it is happening—it's painful! But afterward there will be a peaceful harvest of right living for those who are trained in this way.* Hebrews 12:11

    Why is discipline hard? What have you learned from hard times in your life?

MORE TIME?

- *Because of our love, I prefer simply to ask you. Consider this as a request from me—Paul, an old man and now also a prisoner for the sake of Christ Jesus.* Philemon 1:9

    How do Christians help each other in times of need? How does our pain help us comfort others in pain?

147

Prayer Journal Options

Make a memory about what you read, did, and learned this week.

- Draw a teddy bear and write about comfort.
- Draw a bandage and write about God using doctors to help us.
- Trace your hand (or praying hands) and write why you trust God to answer your prayers.

Family Prayer: Siren Prayers

A siren's blare signals trouble. All of the people involved need prayer, both the responders and those hurt or in trouble. Let sirens call you to pray. Feeling sorry when we know someone is hurting is called *empathy*.

- Pray for the responders—police, medical personnel, firefighters, etc.
- Pray for those who are hurt.
- Pray for the families and loved ones of the people involved.
- Pray for anyone who broke laws or caused accidents. Pray that they will choose to obey and follow Jesus.

Wrap-Up

When you are hurt, pray for comfort and peace.

Why Should I Journal?

Week 34

Family Beatitude: Happy is the family who keeps a prayer journal, for they will have a record of God's answers.

Focus: Prayer journaling

Weekly Bible Verse: *We are writing these things so that you may fully share our joy.* 1 John 1:4

Activity Options

- ☐ Start a prayer journal. Either as a family or individuals. In your journal, describe Jesus and how he is your friend.

- ☐ Add artwork and pictures in your journal. Use stickers to note prayer answers.

- ☐ Trace your hand on pages and write in how you blessed other people with your work.

- ☐ Write about how God answered a special prayer.

Journal Gathering
2 minutes

"It's time to read and celebrate your journals. Bring them here," Mom called to Tilly and Jackson.

They finished up their snacks, grabbed their journals and sat down on the couch.

"Read them silently. If something you wrote gets you excited, share that with us. If you want to keep it to yourself simply give us a thumbs-up sign."

Tilly said, "Wow! I forgot that I prayed for my seeds to grow so I could give the little plants to neighbors. We had marigolds in so many front yards all summer!"

Mom said, "The neighbors still chat about your surprise gift. Mrs. Malone said she prayed for you whenever she looked at her flowers."

Tilly smiled. "My seeds did more than grow flowers. They brought prayers and smiles."

Jackson said, "I like reading about our science experiments with yeast. It helped me understood how Jesus compared yeast to Heaven and also to sin. I like yeast in bread best, and how it makes the flour, and everything grow to make more food for us!"

Mom nodded and said, "What we learn helps us understand more. I like reading how you all prayed over me on Mother's Day. That was a special prayer time for me."

Tilly said, "I drew a lot of the ways we have prayed together. I want to pray Siren Prayers (p. 148) again."

Mom said, "That's a great idea. Let's do it."

Bible Story Connection 3–4 minutes

Read Esther 6:1–11. What did the King do when he couldn't sleep? How did the King's journal help him?

Chat Prompts

- *This is what the LORD, the God of Israel, says: Write down for the record everything I have said to you, Jeremiah.* Jeremiah 30:2

   Jeremiah was a prophet who spoke God's word to the Israelites. How do you listen to God? How is God's Word like a love letter to us?

- *Help me understand the meaning of your commandments, and I will meditate on your wonderful deeds.* Psalm 119:27

   Look up the word *meditate*. How can you think deeply about God's Word? Discuss thinking deeply about God's words and praying about those thoughts.

- *Don't rejoice because evil spirits obey you; rejoice because your names are registered in heaven.* Luke 10:20

   As believers in Jesus, our names are written in God's book in Heaven. What do you think is written in the book? If you had an important book featuring the people in your life, what would you write in it?

MORE TIME?

Prayer Journal Options

Make a memory about what you read, did, and learned this week.

- Draw a book and write why you journal.
- Draw a rainbow and write about adding colors to a prayer journal.
- Draw a heart and write about storing God's words there.

Family Prayer: Prayer Journal

Prayer journaling is a great way to talk with God and recall what you learn from Scriptures.

- Write what you are thinking. No need to be perfect.
- You can divide each day's journal page into sections for praise, thanks, asking God for help, and forgiveness.
- Write your own prayers.
- As you pray, write Scriptures that come into your mind. Reflect on what God's Word is telling you.
- Read over past journal pages to reflect on your spiritual walk with God.

Wrap-Up

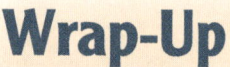

Journaling is a great way to get your thoughts down on paper. Prayer journaling is extra special because after some time, you can reread it and see what prayers have turned into praises!

Should I Keep Praying?

Week 35

Family Beatitude: Happy is the family who watches for God's answers, for they will be satisfied.

Focus: Watching for answers

Weekly Bible Verse: *Rejoice in our confident hope. Be patient in trouble, and keep praying.* Romans 12:12

Activity Options

- ☐ Write prayers or Bible verses on strips of paper. Put them in a bowl on the table where everyone can reach. It's a Scripture snack! Feed your mind with God's Word. Everyone takes a turn choosing a strip of paper and reading it aloud. Use it in place of a snack as a short prayer fast.

- ☐ Let a child hold one end of a short rope (or jump rope) and close their eyes. Shake the rope. Can they feel it? Shake it harder? How is shaking a rope like continuing to pray? God notices when you pray.

- ☐ Take a drive and notice changes in nature or your town. How is God working in these changes?

FAMILY DEVOTION • READ ALOUD

Long Headache 2 minutes

Daniel's head hurt for a few days. His family prayed for God to heal him. The headache continued.

Daniel's mom took him to the doctor, but nothing helped. The headache continued for weeks, months, and then years. Some of the world's best doctors did tests and examined Daniel, but could not find anything that helped. They tried special diets, allergy shots, tests, and medicines, but nothing stopped the constant headache.

Daniel grew up and his family kept praying. Daniel went to another prayer meeting. This time he did not ask for prayer.

"Lord," he prayed quietly in his pew. "If you want me to keep living with this headache, it is OK. But I'd like to pray for other people to be healed." He opened his eyes and looked around the sanctuary. Many people were praying at the front. He walked down the aisle and gently touched a stranger's shoulder.

"Lord, please heal this person of their pain or their fear. Whatever they are going through, I pray that you remind them of your love and your presence in their life. Amen."

As Daniel walked back to his pew, he realized his headache was gone. He went home and thanked God for a few hours with no headache. He waited, but the headache did not return. He waited a month until his mother visited. Then, at church he announced what had happened. He thanked her and everyone for not giving up praying for him.

Bible Story Connection 3–4 minutes

Read about the bleeding woman in Luke 8:43–47 and the angel in Daniel 10:1–14. What do these two stories have in common?

Chat Prompts

- *Keep on asking, and you will receive what you ask for. Keep on seeking, and you will find. Keep on knocking, and the door will be opened to you.* Matthew 7:7

    How is prayer like knocking on a door?

- *Even when you ask, you don't get it because your motives are all wrong—you want only what will give you pleasure.* James 4:3

    Why doesn't God answer every prayer?
    What are selfish prayers?

- *One day Jesus told his disciples a story to show that they should always pray and never give up.* Luke 18:1

    How can you persist in prayer when times get rough?

MORE TIME?

Prayer Journal Options

Make a memory about what you read, did, and learned this week.

- Draw a rope and write about God noticing our prayers.
- Draw someone with a headache and write about God caring about our prayers for healing.
- Draw a door and write what you are praying about.

Family Prayer: Prayer Pit Stop

1. Hang a board to post prayer needs.
2. Post photos of people who need prayer answers.
3. Write notes of prayer needs.
4. When a prayer is answered, take it down and record the answer in a prayer journal. Young children can point to photos and pray with you.

Wrap-Up

God promises to hear every prayer, so always keep praying.

What's the "Golden Rule"?

Week 36

Family Beatitude: Happy is the family who prays the Golden Rule, for they will overcome evil.

Focus: Praying the "Golden Rule" (Luke 6:31)

Weekly Bible Verse: *Do to others as you would like them to do to you.* Luke 6:31

Activity Options

- ☐ On the back of a ruler, write words to remind you how to treat people as you want to be treated (kindness, respect, courtesy, encouragement, etc.) Look at it each night and see if you measured up in doing those things. Alternatively, you could make your own ruler out of colored construction paper.

- ☐ Play a mirror game. Players partner up and take turns imitating motions their partner makes. Talk about mirroring the treatment you want to receive.

- ☐ Play a Golden Rule game. Everyone stands on a start line. The leader asks a question like, "There is only one cookie left so what will you do?" The players call out answers. If a player responded with a Golden Rule answer—like "share it," or "let someone else have it"—they take a step toward the leader. The first person to reach the leader recites, or chooses someone to recite the memory verse.

Praying the Golden Rule 2 minutes

Rowan slammed the door and said, "Asher bullied my friend again. And he tried to bully me, but I walked away."

Aunt Deb hugged Rowan and said, "I think it's Golden Rule prayer time."

"What's that?"

"We've talked about the Golden Rule where Jesus asked us to treat others as we want to be treated. We can list our prayers, but instead of praying them for ourselves, we pray those prayers for Asher."

Rowan nodded. "I'll try that. I want God to give me peace at school with no bullies. And for God to give me good friends."

Aunt Deb added, "I don't know if Asher has good friends or not. My prayer group is praying for his family. His parents are getting a divorce."

"Oh, wow." Rowan thought to herself for a moment before adding, "I'm sorry for Asher. I have a great family; you, Uncle Joey, and little Hudson are all good to me." They prayed over the prayer list, but put in Asher's name for each prayer need.

A few days later, Rowan came home and said, "Asher is different. I said kind things to him."

"What did he do?"

"He made a face, but then walked away instead of saying mean things. Even if we never become friends, I'm going to keep praying for Asher."

Bible Story Connection 3–4 minutes

Read John 13:1–17. How did Jesus gave us an example serving others?

Chat Prompts

- *Don't forget to do good and to share with those in need. These are the sacrifices that please God.* Hebrews 13:16

    How is the Golden Rule about doing good?
    What does it mean to do good?

- *Your love for one another will prove to the world that you are my disciples.* John 13:35

    How does the Golden Rule help us show we love others?

- *Bless those who curse you. Pray for those who hurt you.* Luke 6:28

    Who should you bless or pray for today?

MORE TIME?

Prayer Journal Options

Make a memory about what you read, did, and learned this week.

- Draw a ruler and write the Golden Rule.
- Draw a few inches and write about doing good a little at a time.
- Draw feet and write about Jesus washing the disciples' feet.

Family Prayer: Golden Rule Praying

The Golden Rule is to do for others what you want them to do for you. Vertically trace a ruler on yellow construction paper and mark the inches. Next to each inch mark, write a short prayer you want God to answer.

Now, pray for God to bless a friend or someone else with that request. That's praying the Golden Rule. Pray the Golden Rule for a different person each day. Remember: you can pray this for a bully, too.

Wrap-Up

The Golden Rule is to treat others as you want to be treated.

Why Is Truth Important?

Week 37

Family Beatitude: Happy is the family who promotes honesty, for they will be free.

Focus: Honesty

Weekly Bible Verse: *The LORD is far from the wicked, but he hears the prayers of the righteous.* Proverbs 15:29

Activity Options

- ☐ See how far you can roll marbles. Use a block to stop the marbles. How is sin like a block that stops prayers from getting to God?

- ☐ Drop food coloring into a jar half-filled with water. That's like sin in our life. Pour in ½ to 1 cup of bleach and watch it clean the water. How is the bleach like Jesus? (He cleanses us from sin.)

- ☐ Fill pillowcases with different things like shoes in one and dirty clothes in another. Without revealing what's inside the pillow case, children to rest their heads on each, and guess what's inside. What are pillowcases supposed to be filled with and why? What are our spiritual hearts supposed to be filled with and why?

Brownies 2 minutes

"Brownies! Yummy!" squealed Alice as she grabbed one off the counter. She took a big bite and gagged. "Mia, these taste awful."

"Wow, that's mean," her big sister Mia shot back.

Alice blushed. Sometimes she was too honest and she hurt other people's feelings. "Sorry. Usually your brownies are so good. Did you mix up some ingredients?"

Mia nodded. "I used salt instead of sugar."

"You can't do that," Alice blurted.

"It still has the eggs, chocolate, flour, and oil."

"But the salt ruined it."

"Yeah . . . They say it's what's inside matters," Mia agreed. They were quiet for a moment. Then Mia said softly, "Alice, I think I know why I got confused. I was upset about something. Remember how we learned in Sunday school and admitting when we've done something wrong? And how Jesus can make us clean from our sins? Something's been bothering me . . . You said you couldn't help with the brownies because you had homework. But I heard the theme song to your favorite show playing from your room. I realized you weren't doing homework, and it hurt my feelings that you lied to me."

Alice's face flushed. "I just put it on in the backgr—" she paused and then thought about what Mia said about admitting our sins. She sighed. "Yea, I didn't want to help. I wanted to watch my show. Please forgive me. I can help you make a new batch now." Alice looked at Mia with hopeful eyes.

Mia smiled, "I forgive you. Let's be extra careful with the salt and sugar." Alice smiled.

Bible Story Connection 3–4 minutes

Read Acts 5:1–11. You will not drop dead when you lie to God, but this story shows us the importance of honesty. Why is honesty important to God?

Chat Prompts

- *You will know the truth, and the truth will set you free.* John 8:32

    How do lies trap us and build a web?
    How does the truth set you free?

MORE TIME?

- *The L<small>ORD</small> detests the sacrifice of the wicked, but he delights in the prayers of the upright.* Proverbs 15:8

    How are confession and forgiveness important parts of prayers?

- *The words you speak come from the heart—that's what defiles you.* Matthew 15:18

    "Speaking from your heart" is an expression for saying something honestly. So if you say something negative, it not only hurt the other person, but it hurts you, too. Look up and read the definition of defile. What kinds of words would defile a person? How does what's in our heart (like anger, truth, sin, or love) impact the way you talk?

Prayer Journal Options

Make a memory about what you read, did, and learned this week.

- Draw dirty water and write about sin polluting hearts.
- Draw a stop sign write what things stop prayers.
- Draw a weed and write about pulling out weeds of sin.

Family Prayer: What's Real?

Compare real and fake objects like flowers, food, or money. How did you know which one was true?

Practice honest prayers:

- Praise God for being real and giving us truth.
- Repent of lies you have told.
- Ask God to help you separate truth from lies.
- Yearn to know God's truth and ask God to enlighten your mind.

Wrap-Up

Truth is important because lies lead to trouble. God listens to honest people.

Can Prayer Help Me Change?

Week 38

Family Beatitude: Happy is the family that believes God restores us, for they will have fresh starts.

Focus: Fresh starts

Weekly Bible Verse: *Samuel then took a large stone and placed it between the towns of Mizpah and Jeshanah. He named it Ebenezer (which means "the stone of help"), for he said, "Up to this point the Lord has helped us!"* 1 Samuel 7:12

Activity Options

- [ ] Create a bicycle course with U-turns and bike through it. What does a U-turn mean when you are biking? How can you have a spiritual U-turn?

- [ ] Run fast. When someone yells U-turn, see how fast you can turn around.

- [ ] Drive past a destination and, if it is safe, make a U-turn. How do U-turns help return us to the right path?

Sorry 2 minutes

Jay went to his mom, his head hanging down and math book in his hand. He said, "Mom? I need your help to finish my math assignment."

Mom looked up, surprised. "Didn't you say you'd finished? That's why I let you go out and play ball with the other boys."

Jay said, "Yes, I'm sorry I lied, but I wanted to play ball." He shrugged. "Math doesn't seem that important."

Mom said, "Everything you do uses math. You want be a businessman, so you need to know how money works. That way people can't cheat you."

"But Dad has more degrees than you and he doesn't have a great job. Your job pays the bills."

"I'm thankful I can work, and Dad is studying for a different career. I use math to work my business well. I have to be persistent, keep records, track orders, and balance the money. You're a Christian and need to do what pleases God. That's how to live the best life." Jay nodded. Mom continued, "That's good. God wants you to develop character traits like persistence and honesty. We live in a country with lots of opportunity and freedom, but that also all depends on people being honest and good."

Jay nodded. "Honesty . . . Like not lying about doing your math, right?"

"Right!" Mom added, "If you can't follow through with school, you'll fall away with business, too. You have to have persistence in small things to do greater things."

Jay said, "Mom, I want you to pray with me every day before math. Then God will help me change and do better." She agreed and they prayed a quick prayer before getting to work on Jay's math.

Bible Story Connection 3–4 minutes

Read 1 Samuel 7:1–12. How did God help his people who returned to him? What did Samuel name of the stone? What does the name mean?

Chat Prompts

- *Jeremiah, say to the people, "This is what the Lord says: 'When people fall down, don't they get up again? When they discover they're on the wrong road, don't they turn back?'"* Jeremiah 8:4

    Jeremiah had a message from the Lord to the Israelites. They had sinned, but God wanted them to be encouraged to turn back to him. What does it mean to have a fresh start?

- *As iron sharpens iron, so a friend sharpens a friend.* Proverbs 27:17

    What does it mean to sharpen a friend? It doesn't mean to physically hurt them. It means to make them stronger spiritually. How can you be a good friend and help your friends remain faithful?

- *Turn us again to yourself, O God. Make your face shine down upon us. Only then will we be saved.* Psalm 80:3

    When you reconnect with a friend who you have not seen in awhile, it can be awkward. It is the same with God. When you haven't prayed or read your Bible, being in God's presence can feel uncomfortable. But don't let that discourage you. God wants to give you a fresh start!

MORE TIME?

Prayer Journal Options

Make a memory about what you read, did, and learned this week.

- Draw a stone and write about an Ebenezer.
- Draw a U-turn sign. Write about turning away from making a bad choice.
- Draw a book and write what subject is hardest. Ask family members to pray for you to work diligently.

Family Prayer: Ebenezer Prayers

Use your prayer journal as an Ebenezer (or *stone of help*) memorial. Let it remind you of what God did in the past.

- Flip through pages and read answered prayers.
- Write how God has blessed and helped your family.
- Write how God has changed your heart and mind.
- Keep the journal in plain sight like Samuel did with the Ebenezer stone.
- Pray for needs, believing God will be faithful to answer.
- Listen to the song "Come Thou Fount of Every Blessing."

Wrap-Up

Prayer can change you by making God the focus of your life. Even if you have not prayed in a long time, he will hear your prayer. God love fresh starts!

How Do My Prayers Help Others?

Week 39

> **Family Beatitude:** Happy is the family who prays for others, for they will enlarge God's kingdom.
>
> **Focus:** Praying wider
>
> **Weekly Bible Verse:** *You must grow in the grace and knowledge of our Lord and Savior Jesus Christ. All glory to him, both now and forever! Amen.* 2 Peter 3:18

Activity Options

- [ ] Drop a pebble into water. Watch how the small ripples turn into big ripples. How is a prayer like a ripple effect?

- [ ] Make a cross with two cinnamon sticks and wire-edged ribbon or twist ties. The sweet cinnamon fragrance reflects the sweetness of Jesus' love for us.

- [ ] Draw a picture of a flower, cut it out and glue it to a craft stick. (For extra fun, search online for how to make paper flowers.) Write prayers on the craft stick "stems." Place flowers in a container. Pull one out at a time and pray.

Lost Voice 2 minutes

Bella lost her voice in the summer. This was followed by paralysis that left her unable to walk. Her family prayed for her daily.

Months later, Bella sat by the Christmas tree with her grandma listening to Christmas hymns. On her mini whiteboard she wrote, "I want to sing."

Her grandma replied, "Sing in your heart. God will hear you."

She sighed and wrote, "I want God to hear my voice."

Grandma hugged her close and whispered, "He can hear your voice in your head. He'll like your singing." She cradled Bella and they rocked slightly to the music. Then, Grandma heard a faint whisper. She pulled back, staring at Bella.

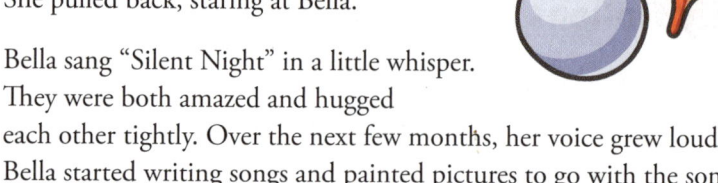

Bella sang "Silent Night" in a little whisper. They were both amazed and hugged each other tightly. Over the next few months, her voice grew louder. Bella started writing songs and painted pictures to go with the songs to bless other people. The following year Bella could use a walker a bit.

Bella rejoiced at the start of the next year, and said it was her best year because she grew in prayer. She learned to hear God's voice and know his will. The family kept praying. That year, two years after she became ill, God healed Bella.

Bible Story Connection 3–4 minutes

Read Luke 18:1–8. What did Jesus say about persistent prayer?

Chat Prompts

MORE TIME?

- *Accept my prayer as incense offered to you, and my upraised hands as an evening offering.* Psalm 141:2

    Incense is a material that smells nice when it's burned. Incense was burned in places of worship and it would rise up to the ceiling and scent the room. How can a prayer be like incense? Discuss how God loves hearing us pray.

- *He was the one who prayed to the God of Israel, "Oh, that you would bless me and expand my territory! Please be with me in all that I do, and keep me from all trouble and pain!" And God granted him his request.* 1 Chronicles 4:10

    Adding more people to your prayer list will grow your "prayer territory." Who can you add to your list of people to pray for?

- *Never stop praying.* 1 Thessalonians 5:17

    Is it easy or hard to prayer persistently? Why or why not?

Prayer Journal Options

Make a memory about what you read, did, and learned this week.

- Draw concentric circles and write about praying for others.
- Draw a cross and write about praying for unbelievers.
- Draw flowers and write about what you have learned about prayer.

Family Prayer: Concentric Circle Prayers

Stand in a tight circle outside. Pray for your family. Step back. Pray for family and friends. Continue stepping back, to make larger circles. Turn outward. Each time pray for a wider group of people:

- Your church community
- Your community
- Your state
- Your country
- Your hemisphere
- The whole world

Wrap-Up

Your prayers help other people by encouraging them to stay faithful and hopeful. God would not tell you to pray if it was useless. Prayers are a personal connection to God.

How Does Praying Together Give Us Power?

Week 40

Family Beatitude: Happy is the family who prays together, for Jesus is with them.

Focus: Praying together

Weekly Bible Verse: *For where two or three gather together as my followers, I am there among them.* Matthew 18:20

Activity Options

- ☐ Make a fruit salad. How do the flavors blend together? How can we blend together in prayer?

- ☐ Make a vine with rope, making loops for people to hold on. Walk around with everyone holding onto the rope vine. How does a real vine grow? Are vines stronger together or alone?

- ☐ One night, turn off all the lights. Light one candle for each person in your family. How does praying together add joy and light?

Darkness and Light 2 minutes

Dad rounded up the kids and said, "Let's all gather in the laundry room." They went in, Mom lit a candle and Dad turned off the lights.

Jonah yelled, "It's too dark. I want the light on."

"It's OK. You sleep in the dark. It won't hurt you." Mom soothed.

"But teddy is with me then."

Dad turned on a little flashlight and said, "Here's a little light you can hold. Do you see how it adds light?" Jonah grabbed the flashlight and held it tight.

Mom passed out candles and they each lit one from the flame on Dad's candle. The room glowed with candlelight.

Dad said, "We added the power of more light. We add a different kind of light when we pray together, an inside glow. A candle produces about thirteen lumens of light. A forty-watt bulb produces about four hundred fifty lumens of light. We need thirty four candles to have the light of a forty-watt bulb like this lamp." Dad flicked on the light.

Jonah breathed a sigh of relief. "I can see better."

Mom said, "We are lights for Jesus and give off a little spiritual light. Jesus is the light of the world and he brightens the world much more than we do."

Jonah's little sister Ellie said, "I'm glad Jesus is with us when we pray."

Bible Story Connection 3–4 minutes

Read Nehemiah 12:27–43. How did the people celebrate the newly rebuilt wall?

Chat Prompts

- *Call on me when you are in trouble, and I will rescue you, and you will give me glory.* Psalm 50:15

    Share times your family prayed together, and God answered your prayers.

MORE TIME?

- *This is my command—be strong and courageous! Do not be afraid or discouraged. For the LORD your God is with you wherever you go.* Joshua 1:9

    Does travel excite you or stress you out? Why? Chat about praying before you travel together.

- *They all met together and were constantly united in prayer, along with Mary the mother of Jesus, several other women, and the brothers of Jesus.* Acts 1:14

    The first believers did not have grand churches to worship in. They met in friends' houses and secret locations and constantly prayed for each other. Do you think their prayers helped their ministry? Why or why not?

Prayer Journal Options

Make a memory about what you read, did, and learned this week.

- Draw a car and write about praying before traveling.
- Draw a vine and write how to cooperate and pray as a family.
- Draw a candle and write about how each family member brightens your days.

Family Prayer: Prayer Vision Board

Use a poster to create a family prayer vision board.

- List prayer goals.
- Add Scriptures that reflect family hopes.
- List virtues to nurture.
- Add family pictures and short prayers that reflect God's call for your family.
- Pray over the things on the vision board.

Wrap-Up

Praying together is powerful because it invites the Holy Spirit, encourages those praying, and helps people desire God's will instead of their own.

How Can I Hear God?

Week 41

Family Beatitude: Happy is the family who hears God's voice, for they will respond.

Focus: Listening to God

Weekly Bible Verse: *My sheep listen to my voice; I know them, and they follow me.* John 10:27

Activity Options

- [ ] Watch a sunrise, be still, and listen:
  - Enjoy the sounds around you.
  - Listen for a Scripture or idea that comes to mind.
  - Make sure that what you hear agrees with the Bible.
  - Share what you heard.
- [ ] Close your eyes and try to recognize sounds. Guess who talks as family members disguise their voices.
- [ ] Place a piece of paper over a raised object (leaf, engraving, penny, etc.). Rub a crayon or pencil over the paper and an impression of the object will appear. God's Word leaves thoughts like impressions, in our mind.

Mom Listened to God 2 minutes

Mom took a deep breath and closed her laptop. Her daughter Stella, who was reading a magazine on the couch, looked up from her article.

"Everything OK? You look stressed."

Mom nodded. "I agreed to come up with art ideas for VBS. The leader just emailed me the theme and asked that I also come up with ideas for the memory verse. I always pray first, and then God fills my head with lots of ideas."

"That's cool."

"It's one way that God talks to me. After a few days I sit with paper and pen and the ideas flow out."

"What's the theme?" Stella asked.

"God Made the Water."

"Well, it's convenient that we live on a Coast Guard base. You can look at stories about water and boats." Then Stella gasped, "Oh! You could use Ryan's favorite verse about hope being our anchor."

Mom smiled thinking of her fiancé. "He'd love that. And I could also use the story of Jesus calming the storm."

A few days later, Stella asked Mom, "Did God give you enough ideas?"

Mom grinned. "Yes. I've got an anchor magnet game in a tuna can, knotted key chains, bracelets crafts, a boat that moves across a paper ocean, and experiments with water drops."

"That sounds like fun."

Bible Story Connection 3–4 minutes

Read 1 Samuel 3:1–21. What happened the first time Samuel heard God's voice? The second time? The third? The fourth?

Chat Prompts

- *Dear friends, do not believe everyone who claims to speak by the Spirit. You must test them to see if the spirit they have comes from God. For there are many false prophets in the world.* 1 John 4:1

  How can you tell if someone is a Christian? How do they act? Dress? Speak? Chat about testing what you hear from others.

MORE TIME?

- *Your own ears will hear him. Right behind you a voice will say, "This is the way you should go," whether to the right or to the left.* Isaiah 30:21

  Isaiah was a prophet who spoke for God. In what ways does God guide your life?

- *My God gave me the idea to call together all the nobles and leaders of the city, along with the ordinary citizens, for registration. I had found the genealogical record of those who had first returned to Judah.* Nehemiah 7:5

  Nehemiah prayed a lot and God spoke to him in different ways. One way was by giving him good ideas. How can praying a lot make it easier to hear God?

Prayer Journal Options

Make a memory about what you read, did, and learned this week.

- Draw an ear and list ways God speaks.
- Draw a picture based on Romans 1:20.
- Draw an object and describe how it sounds.

Family Prayer: Pray and Listen

Read Psalm 46:10 and be silent for a few minutes.

- Think of a-ha moments in your life when you realized something new. How did God use that to teach you something?
- Look up Scriptures that come to mind during your silence. Discuss their meaning. If thoughts are from God, they will be to do good.
- If you believe God spoke, watch for agreement (confirmation) through what someone says, what happens, or what opportunities come up.
- Thank God for always listening to you and ask his help to keep listening for him.

Wrap-Up

Many people in the Bible heard from God by consistently praying for guidance and spending quiet time with God.

Where Is God When I'm Scared?

Week 42

Family Beatitude: Happy is the family who prays when there's danger, for they will remain calm.

Focus: Praying when afraid

Weekly Bible Verse: *"Lord, help!" they cried in their trouble, and he saved them from their distress.* Psalm 107:28

Activity Options

- [ ] Put solar lights in the yard (or watch a video about how solar lights work). How are these solar lights like God's power? (God's power never goes out.)

- [ ] Look at four types of clouds and ways you can pray when you see them.

Name	How It Looks	Weather Pattern	Thank God for
Cumulus	White, puffy, low in sky	Good weather	Sunny days
Cirrus	Wispy low in sky	Brings mist/fog	Comfort in uncertainty
Stratus	Gray lines like blankets	Moist/chilly air	Guidance when life changes
Cumulonimbus	Big, puffy, dark	Storm clouds bring rain	Watering Earth

FAMILY DEVOTION · READ ALOUD

Lightning Storm 2 minutes

Thunder roared and lightning lit the sky. Dad cuddled on the bed with Bailey and Maverick.

Dad said, "The lightning is a type of static electricity. Remember when we made paper circles dance with a ruler?"

Maverick said, "That was cool. You said tiny particles bounced as they bumped into each other."

He nodded and said, "The static electricity caused a little electric charge that attracted the paper circles and they jumped around. The rain drops in the clouds bounce and cause a big electric charge."

"What makes the noise?" Bailey trembled.

"The lightning's electric charge moves faster and heats up the air around it. The air explodes."

Bailey said, "You taught us to count the seconds after the lightning to know how close the lightning is to us."

They saw a lightning bolt and counted two seconds. "It's one mile away." Then it seemed to thunder at the same time the lightning lit the sky. Their bodies were lifted up and then dropped.

Dad said, "The lightning struck our house." He prayed, "Lord, keep us safe."

Dad called the fire department. Firemen came and tested the outlets and appliances. Some were broken by the electrical surge, but they stayed safe.

Bible Story Connection 3–4 minutes

Read Mark 4:35–40. What happened to Jesus and his friends in the storm?

Chat Prompts

- *[Jesus] asked them, "Why are you afraid? Do you still have no faith?"* Mark 4:40

    After Jesus calmed the storm, the disciples were still afraid. Jesus asked them about their faith. Why does Jesus expect us to have faith and not fear?

MORE TIME?

- *So take courage! For I believe God. It will be just as he said.* Acts 27:25

    On his way to Rome for a trial before the emperor, Paul's ship hit a storm. The sailors were terrified. But an angel of the Lord told Paul that everyone would live so he encouraged the crew to be courageous. Have you ever been in a scary situation that required courage? What happened?

- *What a blessing was that stillness as he brought them safely into harbor!* Psalm 107:30

    After a storm, it is a blessing to arrive at a harbor with a still sea. What are ways God comforts you when the storms of life get crazy?

Prayer Journal Options

Make a memory about what you read, did, and learned this week.

- Draw lightning and write about praying for safety.
- Draw clouds and write about praying when you see storm signs.

> **Wrap-Up**
>
> When you are afraid, pray! God is always close by to hear you.

Family Prayer: Bible Story Prayers

Read these two stories about prayer: Mark 4:35–41 and 1 Samuel 17:17–51. As you read, listeners respond with thumbs down for bad part, thumbs up for good parts. Raise your thumbs up higher for each good part or encouragement. Fill out the last column based on another Bible story.

	Mark 4:35–41	1 Samuel 17	
Bad parts	Terrible storm scared disciples	Giant Goliath bullied army	
Good parts	Jesus calmed the storm	David trusted God and killed Goliath	
Praise	Jesus can help us	God is bigger than bullies	
Asking	Help me when I'm scared	Help me with my battle	
More prayer ideas	Help me trust you God	Help me not be afraid of big problem	
Thanks	Thanks for caring for me	Thanks for being bigger than my problem	

How Is God like a Rock?

Week 43

Family Beatitude: Happy is the family who knows God is their rock, for they know God is dependable.

Focus: Dependence on God

Weekly Bible Verse: *Trust in the LORD always, for the LORD GOD is the eternal Rock.* Isaiah 26:4

Activity Options

- [ ] Try to balance a book on an empty toilet-paper tube. Does it work? Now group four or five toilet-paper tubes beside each other and place the book on top. Is it more or less sturdy now? Compare the strength of paper products to rocks.

- [ ] Paint rocks and add words that describe God, or write the words of the memory verse on individual rocks.

- [ ] God gave the Israelites water from a rock (Exodus 17:5–6). Tiny pores in rocks hold water. Gather different rocks. Place each in a container of water. The ones that bubble take in water. See if there's less water when you remove the rock.

Rock Climbing 2 minutes

Dad and Talia buckled their harnesses and approached the rock climbing wall. They clipped their belay devices into the auto belay and clicked them to make sure they were secure.

Dad said, "Let's go. Grab a rock on the wall above your head with your right hand. Then grab one a little higher with your left hand. Next, put one foot on a rock at a time and pull yourself up." Talia nodded.

They began climbing. A few feet off the ground, Talia yelled, "I'm scared. If I place my foot on that little rock I'll fall."

Dad said, "These rocks are strong. They can hold me, so they will hold you."

Talia climbed up high and looked down. She yelled, "Daddy, I'm scared! I'm up too high and I'm dizzy!"

"Look up, not down," Dad said. "You can climb down if you want to or you can let go and lean back in your harness. The auto belay will bring you down safely. See." He pointed to another guy who had just let go of the wall and was caught by his belay.

Talia nodded. She wasn't ready to let go yet. She slowly climbed down. When she felt like she was at a comfortable height, she sat back and kept her feet on the wall. The auto belay caught her and brought her down safely.

At the bottom she laughed, "That was fun, I want to go up again. I'll go higher this time. The rocks are strong. I remember you told me God is like a strong rock."

Dad said, "Yes, God is always strong."

Bible Story Connection 3–4 minutes

Read Joshua 4. What are reasons to make a memorial? Why do rocks make good memorials?

Chat Prompts

- *My victory and honor come from God alone. He is my refuge, a rock where no enemy can reach me.* Psalm 62:7

    How is God like a strong rock? Talk about God being strong and mighty.

- *I am the LORD, and I do not change.* Malachi 3:6

    We serve the same God who did many miracles in the Bible. For thousands of years, he has never changed. How does it make you feel to know that God never changes?

- *Together, we are his house, built on the foundation of the apostles and the prophets. And the cornerstone is Christ Jesus himself.* Ephesians 2:20

    Many houses in the Middle East are build out of rock or stone instead of wood. This is partly because there is more stone available than wood, but it is also because in the hot dry heat, a house made of rock is cooler than a wood one. Discuss rocks used for buildings and how the church is made up of people.

MORE TIME?

Prayer Journal Options

Make a memory about what you read, did, and learned this week.

- Draw rocks and write praises for God our rock.
- Draw a clock or an hourglass. Write about God never changing.
- Draw a building of hearts to show the love of the church.

> **Wrap-Up**
>
> God is like a rock—stable, strong, and trustworthy.

Family Prayer: Prayer Rocks

Talk about properties of rocks and how God is like a rock. Praise God for these qualities.

Scripture	Quality of God
Deuteronomy 32:4	His ways are perfect.
1 Samuel 2:2	No one is holy like him.
2 Samuel 22:2	He is a rock, a fortress who saves us.
2 Samuel 22:3	He is our protector, a refuge of safety.
Psalm 16:8	He is always with me.
Psalm 31:3	He is a fortress who guides us.
Matthew 22:42-44, 1 Peter 2:7	Jesus is the cornerstone and foundation.
1 Peter 2:4	Jesus is the living cornerstone who God values.
1 Peter 2:5	God is a builder, building a temple out of us, his living stones.

How Can I Make God Smile?

Week 44

Family Beatitude: Happy is the family who accepts God's will, for they will prosper.

Focus: Doing what pleases God

Weekly Bible Verse: *Don't act thoughtlessly, but understand what the Lord wants you to do.* Ephesians 5:17

Activity Options

- ☐ Fill bottles with different amounts of water to explore the different sounds they make. Blow across the openings and listen. The blown air vibrates in the bottle and that's what makes sound How high or low the sound is depends on the size of the bottles and the amount of water in them. Is the sound higher or lower in bottles with less space inside for the air to vibrate?

- ☐ Look in a mirror to see yourself. It's actually a reflection. When we show love to others, we reflect God's love.

- ☐ Listen to a seashell or empty glass against your ears. The little chamber that the seashell or glass makes against your ear amplifies the noises around it.

FAMILY DEVOTION · READ ALOUD

Echo Canyon 2 minutes

Jameson and his brother Greyson argued and then started shouting names at each other.

Dad yelled out, "Grab your Bibles and hop in the car. We're taking a trip for today's devotion."

They drove up a mountain. Dad finally stopped and parked the car. They all got out to see the view.

Jameson yelled, "This is cool!" Then he heard his words repeated. "What happened? Did someone copy my words?"

Dad laughed and yelled, "The repeating sounds are echoes!" Dad's words came back too, like the sky rumbled them out loud. "Anyone around can hear your words. Sons, do you want to yell those names you called each other?"

They looked down and shook their heads. Jameson said, "I'm sorry." Greyson repeated Jameson's words and so did the echo.

Dad said, "Think for a minute: what would happen if the words you say were always echoed for everyone to hear?"

Jameson said, "I'd be more careful before I speak."

Dad said, "Let's say things that are good to be echoed." They yelled "Praise God! God loves you! Jesus died for you."

Bible Story Connection 3–4 minutes

Read 1 Kings 19:11–13. Discuss how the prophet Elijah listened to the sounds of nature and then heard God speak.

Chat Prompts

- *John is the man to whom the Scriptures refer when they say, "Look, I am sending my messenger ahead of you, and he will prepare your way before you."* Luke 7:27

    Jesus' cousin, John the Baptist, told many people about Jesus. But some believers were confused and they thought that John was the Messiah. Who did Jesus say that John was? Jesus echoed the Old Testament prophecies and teaching with this verse. This showed he was the true Messiah.

- *For merely listening to the law doesn't make us right with God. It is obeying the law that makes us right in his sight.* Romans 2:13

    Why does it make God smile more when you obey his Word more than echo his Word?

- *May the LORD smile on you and be gracious to you.* Numbers 6:25

    What makes God smile?

MORE TIME?

Prayer Journal Options

Make a memory about what you read, did, and learned this week.

- Draw ears. Write how listening helps you do what God wants.
- Draw a smile and write what pleases God.
- Draw a seashell and write about nature sounds created by God.

Family Prayer: Psalm 136 Echo Prayer

When sound waves bounce off smooth hard surfaces they create an echo. Various Psalms repeat (or echo) phrases. Psalm 136 is one of the most repetitive Psalms which makes memorizing it easy!

Let one person read Psalm 136 and the others echo back the repeated line: "His faithful love continues forever." The first four verses are below:

Give thanks to the LORD, for he is good!
His faithful love endures forever.

Give thanks to the God of gods.
His faithful love endures forever.

Give thanks to the Lord of lords.
His faithful love endures forever.

Give thanks to him who alone does mighty miracles.
His faithful love endures forever.

Wrap-Up

God loves you more than anyone else. The best way to make him smile is to follow his teachings and "love your neighbor as yourself" (Mark 12:31). God wants to bless you every day.

Am I Important to God?

Week 45

Family Beatitude: Happy is the family who knows God values them, for they will live abundantly.

Focus: Valuing yourself the way that God does

Weekly Bible Verse: *Thank you for making me so wonderfully complex! Your workmanship is marvelous—how well I know it.* Psalm 139:14

Activity Options

- ☐ Clean a dirty penny with lemon juice. Read Matthew 6:25–27; Luke 12:6–7. Discuss being more valuable than birds.

- ☐ Show some valuable items (watch, phone, laptop, jewelry, etc.) and discuss how each person is more precious than these things.

- ☐ Use ink or paint to make thumbprints. Using a marker, draw faces, arms, and legs on the thumbprints and make them into artwork. Remember you are "thumb-body" special with unique fingerprints.

You Are Special 2 minutes

Kaley and her Mom browsed the paint color samples in the home improvement aisle. Kaley said, "Wow, there are so many options! I can't wait for my room redo." Mom smiled at her, but it looked a bit forced.

"Are you upset?" Kaley asked.

Mom sighed, "I'm a little sad because before we adopted you, we decorated your room. I know you're not a baby anymore, but I loved those days, too. You're growing up too fast."

Kaley hugged her mom, "It's OK."

Mom said, "We want to bless you again because we love you and want your room to be special and reflect your personality." She pointed at the color samples in Kaley's hand. "You chose two shades of purple—a royal color for a princess of the King." Kaley smiled.

At home, Dad and her sister Everly had moved all the furniture out of her room. Kaley noticed something big in the hallway covered by a sheet. Kaley pulled off the sheet, "Wow! A dressing table with a large mirror."

Dad beamed and said, "We want you to look and know God made you wonderful."

Kaley frowned, "I have too many freckles."

"Those are beauty marks that God sprinkled over you," Dad complimented.

"I know. We need to love everyone, even ourselves, the way God made us."

They moved the dressing table to a corner of the room and stood back to enjoy it.

Bible Story Connection 3–4 minutes

Read Psalm 139. What are some words to describe how valuable we are to God?

Chat Prompts

- *Long ago the L ORD said to Israel: "I have loved you, my people, with an everlasting love. With unfailing love I have drawn you to myself."* Jeremiah 31:3

    Our God keeps his promises. He promised to love the Israelites with an everlasting love. Jesus died for the sins of all people because of God's great love. How do you show love to others?

- *See how very much our Father loves us, for he calls us his children, and that is what we are! But the people who belong to this world don't recognize that we are God's children because they don't know him.* 1 John 3:1

    How does God show you that you are valuable?

- *God showed his great love for us by sending Christ to die for us while we were still sinners.* Romans 5:8

MORE TIME?

You cannot measure God's love for you because he loved you before you even existed! How can you show God's love to others?

Prayer Journal Options

Make a memory about what you read, did, and learned this week.

- Make a thumbprint. Write about being special.
- Draw a bird feather and write about being more valuable than the birds.
- Draw a mirror and write how God sees you and made you.

Family Prayer: Prayer Stretches

Use movement to pray:

- Take a deep breathe. Thank God for breathing life into you (Job 33:4).
- Raise your arms and face to praise God (1 Timothy 2:8).
- Bow down to honor God (Psalm 95:6).
- Stretch out and lift your hands to ask God to fill your needs (Lamentations 3:41).
- Dance as David did to thank God for victory (2 Samuel 6:14).
- Jump to praise God for prayer answers (Acts 3:8).
- Praise the Lord (Psalm 150:6).

Wrap-Up

You are priceless to God.

What Is a Blessing?

Week 46

Family Beatitude: Happy is the family who is thankful for blessings, for they will have enriched lives.

Focus: Blessings from God

Weekly Bible Verse: *"My children, listen to me, for all who follow my ways are joyful."* Proverbs 8:32

Activity Options

- [ ] Put a penny in a jar when anyone in the family is blessed. Count the pennies at the end of a month or year and see how your blessings grew.

- [ ] Before bed, let one person say a family member's name and ask how they were blessed. The person answers and everyone shouts, "Praise the Lord." That person says the next name.

- [ ] Write various blessings on strips of paper (healthy family, kind teachers, good food, etc.). Fill an empty balloon with the blessings strips. Blow up the balloon. Give it to the children to hold up high and pop. The blessings will shower down on them. Alternatively, use a pinata.

FAMILY DEVOTION · READ ALOUD

Blessing Book 2 minutes

Mom and Dad gathered the children on New Year's Day. Mom held up the prayer and praise book that they reread once a year.

She started with the best, worst, and funniest things that happened for the year. "Uncle Manfredo died, I wore my choir outfit inside out during the Christmas pageant, Dad and Uncle Luca bought the same gifts for each other, Gianna's mission trip, and grandparents visiting."

She read the prayer needs they had listed at the beginning of the previous year. "Gianna applying for college, Dad getting a new job, Mateo making it to the state competition in swimming, and for good health for all, especially for Franco's headache to go away. Let's list off some answered prayers."

Mateo offered, "Dad got a great job, but Franco still has that headache."

Gianna called out, "I like my college, and we all stayed healthy."

Dad said, "Time to list this year's prayers. We'll start by writing down the ones not answered yet, like Franco's headache."

They listed the blessings, prayers, and the best, worst, and funniest things from the year. Then Mateo started flipping through past years and read all the funniest times and answered prayers.

Bible Story Connection 3–4 minutes

Read Acts 9:36–42. How did Dorcas bless others?

Chat Prompts

- *Blessed are those who are generous, because they feed the poor.* Proverbs 22:9

    What does it mean to say that it is a blessing to bless others?

- *Through him, God has enriched your church in every way—with all of your eloquent words and all of your knowledge.* 1 Corinthians 1:5

    How has your church blessed you with knowledge and wisdom?

MORE TIME?

- *Give, and you will receive. Your gift will return to you in full—pressed down, shaken together to make room for more, running over, and poured into your lap. The amount you give will determine the amount you get back.* Luke 6:38

    Share stories of how you've been blessed after giving.

Prayer Journal Options

Make a memory about what you read, did, and learned this week.

- Draw a penny and list blessings.
- Draw a balloon or pinata and write about being showered with blessings.
- List the funniest, worst, and best things that happened so far this year.

Family Prayer: Cups of Blessings

Give each child a special blessing cup. Write blessing on strips of paper. Thank God for each blessing. Add other strips whenever you are blessed. Reread them every few weeks, especially when you feel sad or angry.

Wrap-Up

A blessing is an act of kindness for someone else. It makes them feel thankful and at peace. Count your blessings always to stay positive!

Can God Help Us Stop Fighting?

Week 47

Family Beatitude: Blessed is the family who chooses peace, for they will live in harmony.

Focus: Living in peace

Weekly Bible Verse: *Do all that you can to live in peace with everyone.* Romans 12:18

Activity Options

- ☐ Show kids how stain remover works on clothing. Removing a stain is like forgiving someone who hurt you. Sometimes it's easy, other times you really have to scrub at it. Share a time that it was hard to forgive someone.

- ☐ Try singing in harmony and then let everyone sing a different song. What is harmony and what is disharmony?

- ☐ Discuss solving problems with conflict-resolution steps: calm down, talk in a neutral place, let each person share their view, brainstorm possible solutions.

DEEP Time! 2 minutes

Mom walked in the house from the backyard and covered her ears. The TV was blasting. The kids were shouting at each other, stomping their feet, and throwing pillows. Mom yelled, "D.E.E.P. time! Grab a Bible and sit."

Her three children knew that D.E.E.P. time meant to *drop everything and engage in prayer*, but they ignored her. Joseph hurled a pillow at Jeremy, but Mom caught it. "Now!" She said in that forced calm tone, as she used the remote to turn off the TV. The children obeyed. They grabbed their Bibles and gathered in the living room. Mom took a deep breath and so did everyone else. They took several deep breaths until the children started to giggle. Mom then led a prayer for peace. She read Psalm 133 aloud and talked about how trusting God brings harmony.

Jeremy asked, "How is harmony like the olive oil that you read about?"

Mom smiled and said, "The Israelites used oil to anoint someone as a symbol of peace. Some oils help machines when they get stuck."

Jasmine said, "I like it when we live in peace, but when Joseph makes unfair rules, it's no fun." She paused a moment, and then added, "I'm still sorry I argued with my brothers."

Mom said, "Let's take five minutes to read your Bibles, journal, and pray quietly." After five minutes, Mom asked everyone to stop and share any thoughts.

Joseph said, "I read Matthew 5:23–25 where Jesus tells people to make peace before giving a gift to God. I know God wants us to be at peace. I'm sorry I argued."

They held hands to pray.

Bible Story Connection 3–4 minutes

Read Genesis 26:12–25. Discuss how Isaac trusted God for water and worked at keeping peace with people around him.

Chat Prompts

- *Live in harmony with each other. Don't be too proud to enjoy the company of ordinary people. And don't think you know it all!* Romans 12:16

    What are ways that you can live in peace? Some ideas might be to listen well and to respect all people.

- *I have told you all this so that you may have peace in me. Here on earth you will have many trials and sorrows. But take heart, because I have overcome the world."* John 16:33

    How does Jesus give you inner peace?

- *God blesses those who work for peace, for they will be called the children of God.* Matthew 5:9

    Discuss who in the family has been a peacemaker lately. Applaud them.

MORE TIME?

Prayer Journal Options

Make a memory about what you read, did, and learned this week.

- Draw a well. Write about ways to react to someone being mean.
- Draw a heart with a cross. Write about entrusting your problems to Jesus.
- Draw a Bible and write about D.E.E.P.

Family Prayer: D.E.E.P. Time

D.E.E.P. represents "Drop Everything and Engage in Prayer." It's good to do in a crisis or when children are arguing as it causes everyone to pause. Stop, call D.E.E.P. time, and gather together.

- Begin with having everyone take slow breaths.
- Pray for peace and harmony.
- Share a verse about peace like John 16:33. Use a verse from this chapter, or find one in a concordance.
- Let everyone silently read for five minutes or journal. Share any special thoughts from the readings or journaling. Pause and pray as you read.
- Calmly discuss the problems and pray for the help of Jesus, the Prince of Peace, to solve problems.
- Take turns praying about peace in your home.

Wrap-Up

God brings peace. Be a peacemaker.

How Can I Learn about God?

Week 48

Family Beatitude: Happy is the family who prays for wisdom and knowledge, for they become wiser.

Focus: Knowledge of God

Weekly Bible Verse: *True wisdom and power are found in God; counsel and understanding are his.* Job 12:13

Activity Options

- [ ] Place two or three bowls of different liquids (colored water, corn syrup, olive oil, etc.) on the table. Use sponges and paper towels to see how they soak up (absorb) the different liquids. How can you soak up Bible knowledge?

- [ ] Name some ways that you could sacrifice you time or belongings. Some ideas are shutting off electronic devices for fifteen minutes to pray, letting someone else go first, giving up snacks or dessert, or freely doing extra chores.

- [ ] At meals ask each person, "What did you learn today?"

Teaching about Abraham 2 minutes

Darlene found her foster children dressed in bathrobes with sticky, white goop in their hair.

"Darius, what did you put in your hair? And why?"

Darius grinned, "I wanted to teach Aaliyah about Abraham and Sarah. We dressed up, but we needed to look old. I used the white stuff you use when you change diapers."

Darlene said, "I'm glad you like teaching about God, but you need to ask me what will work to look old. That will be hard to get out."

Darlene washed their hair several times as Darius continued to share about Abraham. He said, "After a long time of waiting for a baby, three strangers came to see Abraham. Abraham fed them and they told him Sarah would have a baby. I think we should have a tea party, so you'll know how to be good to visitors."

Aaliyah said, "Tea party. Yes."

Darius said, "God told Abraham that his children and their children would have many children. They would be a nation with more people than stars in the sky. Mom, we need to stay awake and see the stars. We can try to count them."

Darlene nodded, "We'll find a night when you can sleep late the next morning. I'm happy you remember what we read in the Bible."

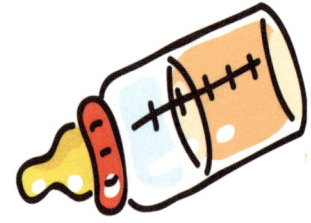

Bible Story Connection 3–4 minutes

Read 2 Chronicles 1:6–11 and 1 Kings 4:29–31.
Why did God give Solomon so much wisdom?

Chat Prompts

- *All the believers devoted themselves to the apostles' teaching, and to fellowship, and to sharing in meals (including the Lord's Supper), and to prayer.* Acts 2:42

    How does your family share faith and food?

- *The people of Berea were more open-minded than those in Thessalonica, and they listened eagerly to Paul's message. They searched the Scriptures day after day to see if Paul and Silas were teaching the truth.* Acts 17:11

    What are different ways to study the Bible?

- *For the LORD grants wisdom! From his mouth come knowledge and understanding.* Proverbs 2:6

    What does wisdom mean? Pray together for wisdom.

MORE TIME?

Prayer Journal Options

Make a memory about what you read, did, and learned this week.

- Draw stars and write about God's faithfulness.
- Draw a sponge and write something you "soaked up" or learned.
- Draw a teacup and write about sharing with visitors.

> **Wrap-Up**
>
> Learn about God by reading the Bible and praying.

Family Prayer: Creeds

A creed is a statement or declaration of basic truths about God. Creeds are important to know because they unite all believers. It's from the Latin word *credo* that means *I believe*. Look up these verses and use them as prayer statements of what you believe.

Scripture	Creed
1 Corinthians 8:6	"There is one God, the Father, by whom all things were created, and for whom we live. And there is one Lord, Jesus Christ, through whom all things were created, and through whom we live."
Philippians 2:9–11	"God elevated him to the place of highest honor and gave him the name above all other names, that at the name of Jesus every knee should bow, in heaven and on earth and under the earth, and every tongue declare that Jesus Christ is Lord, to the glory of God the Father."
Deuteronomy 6:4 (Jews pray this every morning and evening.)	"Listen, O Israel! The Lord is our God, the Lord alone."

How Can I Share My Faith?

Week 49

Family Beatitude: Happy is the family who shares their faith, for they will grow God's kingdom.

Focus: Sharing faith

Weekly Bible Verse: *Come and listen, all you who fear God, and I will tell you what he did for me.* Psalm 66:16

Activity Options

- ☐ Make colored beaded necklaces, bracelets, or key chains to share faith. Put a black bead for sin, a red bead for Jesus dying to save us, a yellow bead for new life, an orange bead for the fire of the Holy Spirit, and a green bead for growing your faith. Share it with an unbeliever.

- ☐ Decorate a treasure box. Let children fill it with reminders of Bible stories (a small rock for David and Goliath, a toy boat for Noah, etc.). Use it to share the stories with friends.

- ☐ Do acts of kindness as sacrifices. When someone thanks you for something, say you did it to share God's love.

The Bread Plate 2 minutes

The dinner table was full of new neighbors. Mrs. Oh took a roll and said, "What an interesting plate." It had a bread design and the words *Jesus Is the Bread of Life*.

Eva said, "That's our bread plate. It helps us remember to thank God for our food."

Mr. Oh said, "Oh, well, we don't go to church."

Eli said, "I like going to church. We hear stories about Jesus. We're good friends and he answers my prayers. When I do wrong things, Jesus forgives me."

Eva said, "Jesus is the only one who can forgive us because he died to pay the price for our sins. Jesus loves everyone! You just need to believe he died and rose again to forgive your sins. Then you'll go to Heaven."

Mr. Oh laughed, "That sounds too easy."

Eli said, "It's easy so that everyone can be part of God's family."

After the guests left, Dad said, "I'm so proud of the way you both shared your faith."

Eli furrowed his brows. "We just explained our bread plate."

"Yes, and that let you talk about prayer and Jesus. That's sharing faith."

Eva said, "I'm praying that Mr. and Mrs. Oh will believe. Maybe they'll even come to church!"

Bible Story Connection 3–4 minutes

At Pentecost, Peter spoke boldly about his faith in Jesus. Read Acts 2:1–4,14–21,38–41. How did Peter share his faith? Sharing your faith is called a *testimony*.

Chat Prompts

- *Therefore, go and make disciples of all the nations, baptizing them in the name of the Father and the Son and the Holy Spirit.* Matthew 28:19

    Missionaries travel the world to share their faith. Who are some that you have heard of? Some examples might be Jim and Elisabeth Elliot, Amy Carmichael, Hudson Taylor, the Apostle Paul, etc.

- *After seeing him, the shepherds told everyone what had happened and what the angel had said to them about this child.* Luke 2:17

    How did the shepherds share their joy about Jesus?

- *Everyone who acknowledges me publicly here on earth, I will also acknowledge before my Father in heaven.* Matthew 10:32

    Why is it important to God that you share your faith?

MORE TIME?

Prayer Journal Options

Make a memory about what you read, did, and learned this week.

- Draw the colored beads from the activity on page 209 and write what each color represents.
- Draw a bread plate and write about sharing faith at meals.
- Draw pretzels and write about pretzel prayers (explained below).

Wrap-Up

Share your faith.

Family Prayer: Pretzel Prayers

On a paper plate, write *Jesus is the Bread of Life*. Fill it with pretzels and share the facts below as you snack:

What to Say	What to Do
In 610, a monk twisted and baked scraps of dough into the shape of arms folded in prayer.	Cross your arms and praise God.
He used the Latin word "pretiola" which means "little reward." They were given to children when they learned to pray.	Family members take turns thanking God for little blessings. Give each a pretzel at the end of their prayer.
The three empty holes symbolize the trinity.	Praise each person of the Trinity.
Pretzels were a sign of unity. They were served at weddings. This is where the saying "tying the knot" comes from.	Pray for your family to be united.
In Germany, children found hidden pretzels on Good Friday. They were served with two boiled eggs nestled in the large holes to represent rebirth at Easter.	Thank God for saving you.

What Does "Glory to God" Mean?

Week 50

Family Beatitude: Happy is the family who celebrates God's glory, for they will be lights for God.

Focus: Celebrating God's glory

Weekly Bible Verse: *Glory to God in highest heaven, and peace on earth to those with whom God is pleased.* Luke 2:14

Activity Options

- [ ] Set up a nativity set. Where is Jesus usually placed in a nativity scene? Why?

- [ ] Look at the big night sky and stars, or look up pictures online. God is bigger than the sky. How do you feel when you think about God being bigger than everything?

- [ ] Look at something very tiny, like an insect and discuss how God created intricate things, too.

Christmas Cheer 2 minutes

It was Christmas decorating day in the Martinez house, but before they unpacked anything, they had a tradition to uphold.

Mama read the story of Jesus' birth. Then she said, "Glory to God in the highest!" Everyone echoed her words.

Papa said turned to his oldest son and said, "Antonio, help me with the lights, please." Antonio held onto the end of the strand as Papa placed lights on the tree. Antonio plugged in the cord and the tree lit up. Carmen and Santiago clapped their hands.

Mama said, "Jesus is the light of the world."

Everyone shouted, "Glory to God in the highest!"

Everyone took turns adding ornaments and sang "Vamos, Pastores, Vamos!" ("Let's Go, Shepherds, Let's Go!").

Carmen pulled out stockings from the boxes of decorations. She said, "Stockings remind us that our hearts are filled with the Holy Spirit and God's love. Glory to God in the highest!"

They munched on cookies as they continued to decorate.

As they finished Santiago said, "I love how everything sparkles and changes the house to look like a big party. It's fun to give glory to God."

Bible Story Connection 3–4 minutes

Read Luke 2:8–18. How did the first people to hear the news of Jesus' birth celebrate? Discuss the angel's words, God's glory, and how shepherds celebrated Jesus.

Chat Prompts

- *The heavens proclaim the glory of God. The skies display his craftsmanship.* Psalm 19:1

    How does the sky and universe reflect God's great power and creative imagination?

MORE TIME?

- *In the same way, let your good deeds shine out for all to see, so that everyone will praise your heavenly Father.* Matthew 5:16

    How does sharing our faith and following Jesus help others see God at work?

- *For God, who said, "Let there be light in the darkness," has made this light shine in our hearts so we could know the glory of God that is seen in the face of Jesus Christ.* 2 Corinthians 4:6

    What does it mean to have light in our hearts? How does light in our hearts help us know God's glory?

Prayer Journal Options

Make a memory about what you read, did, and learned this week.

- Draw bright lights and angels. Write about God's glory and the shepherds (Luke 2:9).
- Draw stars and write about God being bigger than the sky.
- Draw baby Jesus and write "Glory to God."

Wrap-Up

Glorify God by singing worship songs, sharing your faith, praying often, and serving others.

Family Prayer: God's Glory

Sing or shout out the words the angels sang to celebrate God's glory: "Glory to God in the highest!"

What to Say	What to Do
Jesus is the light of the world (John 8:12).	Put up Christmas lights.
Jesus is the greatest, most valuable gift (John 3:16).	Wrap gifts.
God is the Creator who made everything, and all creation reflects God's glorious deeds (Romans 1:20).	Hang ornaments on a Christmas tree.
God is eternal (Deuteronomy 33:27).	Hang an evergreen wreath to represent eternity.
Jesus guides us as our shepherd (John 10:11).	Put out candy canes, shaped like a shepherd's staff.
Celebrate Jesus' birthday (Luke 2:7).	Light a birthday candle and sing "Happy Birthday" to Jesus.

What Should I Do When God Answers My Prayers?

Week 51

Family Beatitude: Happy is the family who rejoices at prayer answers, for they will keep praying.

Focus: Celebrate that God answers prayers.

Weekly Bible Verse: [God said,] *I will answer them before they even call to me. While they are still talking about their needs, I will go ahead and answer their prayers!* Isaiah 65:24

Activity Options

- [ ] Use a ball to play a team game. What does it mean to be a team player with God in prayer?

- [ ] On an old beach ball, write words with a marker (names, things God created, names for God, actions, etc.). Toss the ball. The catcher must read the word closest to their right thumb and thank God for or pray about the word.

- [ ] Practice ball skills for soccer, baseball, basketball, or other ball sports. How do you develop skill and strength? Pray to develop persistence, grateful hearts, and talents.

Shooting Hoops 2 minutes

Liam was shooting hoops in the driveway when Aunt Kelly got home from work.

"Hey!" Liam waved when he saw her car. "Wanna play?" He pointed to the basketball. Aunt Kelly nodded and parked on the street. They worked on dribbling, snatching the ball, and shooting baskets.

When Liam missed the hoop again, he sighed, "I'm not very good."

Aunt Kelly said, "It takes practice. I used to be better but I'm out of practice and out of shape." She laughed. "If we do this every day, we'll both improve."

A week later, Liam was able to make a basket more often. Two weeks later, Liam could dribble the ball for thirty seconds.

Liam said, "Aunt Kelly, you were right. I'm getting better with practice. You are, too. You make a basket almost every time."

Aunt Kelly high-fived him. She said, "You ran fast while dribbling. Practicing helps. Practice helps with lots of things." She snapped her fingers. "Like with prayer. As we have prayed together all year, you've become more and more comfortable talking with God."

Liam nodded, "Prayer is easier once I gave all my hurt and anger to him. I like talking to God."

Aunt Kelly grinned. "That's something to celebrate! Let's go get a snack. And some water!"

Bible Story Connection 3–4 minutes

Read Nehemiah 12:27–31,43. How did the people celebrate after completing the wall? What does it mean that the celebration was a dedication? To whom was the wall dedicated?

Chat Prompts

MORE TIME?

- *David danced before the Lord with all his might, wearing a priestly garment.* 2 Samuel 6:14

    David was so happy that he danced before God. Turn on some praise music and dance for the Lord. Praise him for all the blessings he has given you.

- *The Lord is my strength and shield. I trust him with all my heart. He helps me, and my heart is filled with joy. I burst out in songs of thanksgiving.* Psalm 28:7

    Have you ever experienced joy after a prayer was answered? Chat about joy that comes with praying and answers to prayer.

- *As soon as I pray, you answer me; you encourage me by giving me strength.* Psalm 138:3

    How does prayer strengthen your faith and trust in God? Rejoice that praying helps you.

Prayer Journal Options

Make a memory about what you read, did, and learned this week.

- Draw something to represent an answered prayer.
- Draw a wall and write about Nehemiah's people repairing, dedicating, and celebrating the wall of Jerusalem.

Family Prayer: Ball Prayers

Form a circle. Use a ball to prompt prayers.

What to Say	What to Do with the Ball
Praise God for _____.	Throw it high and catch it.
Thank God for his forgiveness.	Bounce it.
Share a blessing and thank God for it.	Toss it to another player.
Thank God for rolling with you.	Roll it to another player.
Say a prayer for a player.	Dribble around the person you pray for.
Pray for persistence.	Try to balance it on a body part (head, knee, elbow, etc.).

Wrap-Up

When God answers your prayers, celebrate! Let others know of your incredible blessing.

What Does It Mean to Commit to God?

Week 52

Family Beatitude: Happy is the family committed to God, for God will give them the desires of their hearts.

Focus: Commitment to God

Weekly Bible Verse: *Commit your actions to the Lord, and your plans will succeed.* Proverbs 16:3

Activity Options

- [ ] Celebrate completing this book and your commitment to pray as a family! Search online for a graduation template or certificate. Print one for each family member to fill out.

- [ ] Read Psalm 100:2 which is about worshiping the Lord. Parade around your house or a room singing songs of praise. Repeat this verse at the beginning and end.

- [ ] Make a plaque to put over your door with the words from Joshua 24:24 or your own words.

Serve with Hands and Feet 2 minutes

"Mimi, how can we be the feet and hands of Jesus? Are we going to get holes in our hands, too?" Gabriella asked with a trembling voice.

Mimi laughed, "When Pastor Elliot said that, he didn't mean literally. He meant that we should serve with our hands and feet the same way Jesus did. He healed people with his hands, and he traveled to spread the Good News with his feet."

Gabriella breathed a sigh of relief. Her brother, Owen, was deep in thought. He said, "Could we make sandwiches for the homeless? They had a sign-up sheet at the Welcome Desk. We could do it once a month."

Gabriella clapped her hands. "So we make the sandwiches with our hands and we can use our feet to take them to church. Will we pass them out?"

"Nice idea," Mimi agreed, "But we cannot go to pass them out to the homeless because you are both too young. But we can provide the sandwiches."

"We want to share our faith, so how can we do that?" Owen objected.

Mimi thought for a moment. "We could use markers to write notes on the sandwich bags." She suggested.

"We could draw hearts and write God loves you," said Gabriella.

"Sounds like a great plan, kiddos!"

Bible Story Connection 3–4 minutes

Read Joshua 24:13–27. What did the Israelites promise God? What did the stone signify?

Chat Prompts

- *The people said to Joshua, "We will serve the Lord our God. We will obey him alone."* Joshua 24:24

    What habits can you put in place so that you can pray together as a family in the coming year? What were your favorite family prayer methods in this book?

- *This is my command: Love each other.* John 15:17

    What does Jesus want us to do as his followers? How can you show love as a family today?

- *Take delight in the Lord, and he will give you your heart's desires.* Psalm 37:4

    Why is it a big deal to follow God? What have been some of your favorite blessings this year?

MORE TIME?

Prayer Journal Options

Make a memory about what you read, did, and learned this week.

- Write ways to serve God and draw hands and feet.
- Draw a heart and write a desire of your heart.
- Write a note to God that you want to serve him.

Family Prayer: Dedication and Commitment

1. Read what Jesus said were greatest commandments (Matthew 22:36–40).
2. Agree to serve and let everyone echo these words:

   - Let us serve God with our hands.
   - Let us be the feet of Jesus to go and serve others.
   - Let our tongues and mouths share God's love.
   - Let us serve God with our ears open to listen to his guidance.
   - Let us serve God with all our hearts, minds, and souls.
   - We will serve the Lord and dedicate ourselves to following God.

3. Have a special party to celebrate your commitment as a family.

Wrap-Up

Committing to God means that you promise to serve him only. Agree to serve the Lord as a family.